DK EYEWITNESS

T0043470

TOP **10**
VALENCIA

Top 10 Valencia Highlights

The Top 10 of Everything

CONTENTS

Valencia Area by Area

Streetsmart

Within each Top 10 list in this book, no hierarchy of quality or popularity is implied. All 10 are, in the editor's opinion, of roughly equal merit.

Title page, front cover and spine *Spectacular view over the old Valencia*
Back cover, clockwise from top left *High altar, La Catedral; the Centro Histórico at sunset; kitesurfing on Playa de las Palmeres; Palau de les Arts Reina Sofia; El Miguelete tower and La Catedral seen from Plaza Reina*

The rate at which the world is changing is constantly keeping the DK Eyewitness team on our toes. While we've worked hard to ensure that this edition of Valencia is accurate and up-to-date, we know that opening hours alter, standards shift, prices fluctuate, places close and new ones pop up in their stead. So, if you notice we've got something wrong or left something out, we want to hear about it. Please get in touch at **travelguides@dk.com**

Welcome to
Valencia

Sandwiched between the Mediterranean Sea and the fertile fields of La Huerta, Valencia has a sublime location. Few cities have such an enjoyable mix of medieval streetscapes and cutting-edge architecture, where Modernista markets rub shoulders with futuristic performance venues. The food is fantastic, the nightlife is legendary. With Eyewitness Top 10 Valencia, it's yours to explore.

Valencia is compact and intimate and feels more like a cluster of historic neighbourhoods than the dynamic, innovative city that it has become. The **Centro Histórico** is a warren of backstreets, at their most dense around the **Barrio del Carmen**. High-end fashion boutiques line the Neo-Classical boulevards of upmarket **L'Eixample**, while hipster **Ruzafa** offers a treasure trove of vintage shops and some of the most interesting restaurants in the city. Shabby chic **El Cabanyal**, a former fishing quarter of colourfully tiled townhouses, backs onto some of the finest city beaches in Spain.

You can trace Valencia's history in **La Catedral** – the cathedral's style spans Romanesque to Baroque; visit the **Museo Nacional de Cerámica**; or cycle through the **Jardín del Turia**, a ribbon of green space that is emblematic of the city's capacity for change. Shop for groceries in the beautiful **Mercado Central** or gaze in wonder at the sheer audacity of the **Ciudad de las Artes y las Ciencias**.

Whether you're coming for a weekend or a week, our Top 10 guide brings together the best of everything the city can offer, from **Parroquia San Nicolás**'s frescoed ceiling to the UNESCO World Heritage Site of **La Lonja de la Seda**. The guide has useful tips throughout, from seeking out what's free to getting off the beaten track, plus eight easy-to-follow itineraries, designed to help you visit a clutch of sights in a short space of time. Add inspiring photography and detailed maps, and you've got the essential pocket-sized travel companion. **Enjoy the book, and enjoy Valencia.**

Clockwise from top: El Miguelete tower in La Catedral, entrance to Mercado Central, Ubik Café, Palacio del Marqués de Dos Aguas, Museo de Bellas Artes overlooking Jardín del Turia, detail of the Museu de les Ciències, street art on Bed & Bike shop

Exploring Valencia

There is so much to see in and around Valencia, from historical sights and museums to cutting-edge buildings and hilltop towns. Whether you are here for a weekend or have an extra couple of days to explore more of the region, these two- and four-day itineraries will help you make the most of your visit.

The Museo de Bellas Artes has an outstanding collection of medieval art, including these sumptuous altarpieces.

Jardín del Turia
Túria Metro
Café del Duende
Barrio del Carmen
Valencia Bikes
CYCLE
Parroquia de San Nicolás
Torres de Quart
La Lonja de la Seda
Mercado Central
Bus 35 terminal
METRO
Plaza del Ayuntamiento
Xàtiva Metro
Estación del Norte
TRAIN

0 metres	600
0 yards	600

to Xàtiva
60 km (38 miles)

Two Days in Valencia

Day ❶
MORNING
Climb up the Torres de Quart for an overview of the **Barrio del Carmen** *(see pp12–13)*, then pay a visit to the Parroquia de San Nicolás before wandering the labyrinth of lanes that make up this medieval quarter.

AFTERNOON
Cross the **Puente de la Trinidad** *(see p22)* to the **Museo de Bellas Artes** *(see pp30–33)*. After admiring the works by Joaquín Sorolla and other Valencian artists, join the locals for a stroll through the neighbouring **Jardín del Turia** *(see pp22–3)*.

Day ❷
MORNING
Start at the 13th-century **La Catedral** *(see pp14–17)* and from there walk to **La Lonja de la Seda** *(see pp20–21)* before grabbing a bite to eat at the Central Bar in Valencia's Modernista **Mercado Central** *(see pp18–19)*.

AFTERNOON
Visit the futuristic **Ciudad de las Artes y las Ciencias** *(see pp26–9)* Spend the day exploring the fascinating science museum, catch a film at Hemisfèric and finish the day with a cocktail at L'Umbracle Terraza.

Four Days in Valencia

Day ❶
MORNING
Start the day with an ice-cold *horchata* (a local drink made from tiger nuts) at **Horchatería de Santa Catalina** *(see p84)*, then visit the Gothic **La Catedral** *(see pp14–17)*.

AFTERNOON
After a tapas lunch in the Centro Histórico, enjoy a walk around the eclectic gardens of **Jardines del Real** *(see p104)* before touring the **Museo de Bellas Artes** *(see pp30–33)*. Watch an evening flamenco show at **Café del Duende** *(see p106)*.

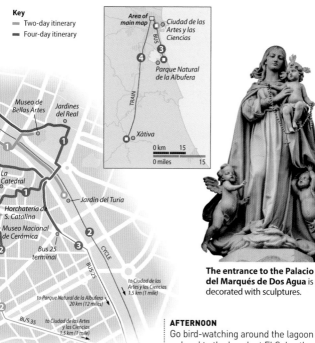

Key
— Two-day itinerary
— Four-day itinerary

The entrance to the Palacio del Marqués de Dos Agua is decorated with sculptures.

AFTERNOON
Go bird-watching around the lagoon or head to the beach at El Saler, then take a boat trip across the lake.

Day ❹
MORNING
Catch the train from the Modernista **Estación del Norte** (see p95) to Xàtiva (see p38–9) and spend the morning exploring the town's castle.
AFTERNOON
Wander Xàtiva's Old Town, visiting the Colegiata Basílica de Santa María or the Museo de l'Almudí.

The Neo-Classical Town Hall sits on the west side of Plaza del Ayuntamiento.

Day ❷
MORNING
Catch the early morning bustle at the **Mercado Central** (see pp18–19), then peruse the ceramics collections at the **Museo Nacional de Cerámica** (see p88), housed in the Baroque Palacio del Marqués de Dos Aguas.
AFTERNOON
Admire the grand buildings on **Plaza del Ayuntamiento** (see p51) on the way to Xàtiva metro station. After picking up rental bikes from Valencia Bikes near Turia station, cycle through the **Jardín del Turia** (see pp22–3) to the **Ciudad de las Artes y las Ciencias** (see pp26–9).

Day ❸
MORNING
Visit **La Lonja de la Seda** (see pp20–21) before diving into the **Barrio del Carmen** (see pp12–13). Catch the No 25 bus to the **Parque Natural de la Albufera** (see pp36–7) for lunch at a paella restaurant in El Palmar.

Top 10 Valencia Highlights

The flamboyant façade of
La Catedral (Valencia Cathedral)

🔟 Valencia Highlights

The third-largest city in Spain after Madrid and Barcelona, Valencia has world-class museums, fabulous festivals, a dynamic restaurant scene, great shopping and some of the best city beaches in Europe. Just outside the city are the wetlands of the Parque Natural de la Albufera, where you can go bird-watching, take a boat trip and have lunch at the best paella restaurants in the world.

❶ Barrio del Carmen
Framed by the remnants of Valencia's city walls, the Barrio del Carmen is a jumble of tightly packed streets, art galleries, ancient churches and trendy vintage boutiques (see pp12–13).

La Catedral ❷
The cathedral is one of the city's most distinctive buildings and spans six centuries of architectural styles. Inside, the Capilla del Santo Cáliz reputedly harbours the Holy Grail among its treasures (see pp14–17).

❸ Mercado Central
Scour the stalls for delicious seafood, dry-cured hams and freshly picked vegetables at this remarkable Modernista market, the largest of its kind in Europe (see pp18–19).

La Lonja de la Seda ❹
If one building defines the flourishing of art in Valencia in the 15th to 16th centuries, it is La Lonja de la Seda, an epic work of Gothic architecture and a UNESCO World Heritage Site (see pp20–21).

❺ Jardín del Turia
Follow the locals' lead and walk, jog or cycle through the gardens that follow the course of the Río Turia (see pp22–3).

6 Ciudad de las Artes y las Ciencias

Zany, astonishing, pioneering, colossal – Santiago Calatrava's sensational City of Arts and Sciences is all of these and more *(see pp26–9)*.

7 Museo de Bellas Artes

The 17th-century Collegio Seminario de San Pío V makes a suitably grand setting for this esteemed museum of fine arts, noted for its Valencian Gothic art and collection of paintings by Joaquín Sorolla *(see pp30–33)*.

8 Las Fallas

Valencianos have celebrated the arrival of spring with this splendid festival of pyrotechnics and tradition since at least the 1750s. Artists spend a year creating their elaborate, cartoonish *fallas* monuments, only to set them alight on 19 March *(see pp34–5)*.

9 Parque Natural de la Albufera

This wonderland of wetlands has a huge lake, lagoons, rice fields and forested dunes *(see pp36–7)*.

10 Xàtiva

Making an excellent day trip from Valencia, this picturesque town has a dramatic ridgetop castle with wonderful panoramic views of the surrounding area *(see pp38–9)*.

⭐ Barrio del Carmen

Encompassing a tangle of narrow streets and cobbled alleyways in the northwest corner of Valencia's Centro Histórico, this district – Barri del Carme in Valencian – is the city's oldest and most atmo-spheric. It sprang up over 1,000 years ago and retains the feel of a medieval neighbourhood. The barrio is one of the city's trendiest areas, with once crumbling palaces and townhouses transformed into cafés and restaurants. The nightlife here is legendary, too, with an eclectic range of bars and clubs.

Map of Barrio del Carmen

A typical narrow street in Barrio del Carmen

1 Torres de Quart

Styled on Naples's Castel Nuovo, this 15th-century gateway still bears the marks of French cannon fire from the Peninsular War. Climb to the top of the tower for great views.

2 L'ETNO (Museo de Etnologia)

The popular L'ETNO, which explores local culture and society across three exhibitions, was voted European Museum of the Year in 2023.

3 Casa-Museo José Benlliure

The family home of José Benlliure y Gil (1858–1937) gives a good idea of what life was like in a 19th-century Valencian house. Many of the artist's works are on display.

4 Portal de la Valldigna

One of the few surviving remnants of Valencia's old city walls, this gateway was built in 1400 to connect the Arab quarter with the city centre.

5 Parroquia de San Nicolás

Tucked away off Calle Caballeros, this beautiful 15th-century Gothic church is known as the Valencian Sistine Chapel thanks to the magnificent 17th-century frescoes that cover every inch of its vaults. The interior is gleaming after a meticulous restoration removed over 200 years of candle smoke (left).

6 Torres de Serranos

Built at the end of the 14th century, the Torres de Serranos marked the north entrance to the old city **(left)** and were part of the city walls, which were dismantled in 1865.

7 Museo del Corpus

This museum inside Casa de las Rocas houses the Giants and Bigheads that form part of the Corpus Christi parades and a dozen *rocas* (rocks) – processional carriages with biblical figures.

8 Centro del Carmen

The monastery that gave Barrio del Carmen its name is now a centre of contemporary culture, hosting concerts, films and lectures, as well as temporary exhibitions.

9 Calle de los Colores

The walls of Calle Moret serve as a canvas for Valencian street artists such as Luis Lonjedo and Deih. Look out for paintings like *Bridge in Venice* and *Kiss*.

CASA DE LOS GATOS

Befitting the district's alternative character, Calle Museo is home to a very unusual little house. Built into the wall halfway along the street and just a couple of feet tall, the building has its own tiled roof, balcony and miniature fountain. According to local legend, the so-called "House of Cats" was left behind by the former owner as a refuge for the city's feral felines.

10 Institut Valencià d'Art Modern (IVAM)

Founded in 1989, IVAM was Spain's first contemporary art museum **(above)**. It focuses on the Cubist sculptor Julio González (1876–1942) and the Impressionist painter Ignacio Pinazo (1849–1916).

NEED TO KNOW

MAP K1

Torres de Quart: c/Guillem de Castro 89; open 10am–7pm Tue–Sat, 10am–2pm Sun; adm €2, free Sun

L'ETNO (Museo de Etnologia): c/Corona 36; open 10am– 8pm Tue–Sun; adm €2, free Sat & Sun; https://letno.dival.es

Casa-Museo José Benlliure: c/de Blanquerías 23; 963 911 662; open 10am–

1:30pm & 4–6pm Tue, 10am– 2pm & 3–7pm Wed–Sat, 10am–2pm Sun; adm €2, free Sun

Parroquia de San Nicolás: c/Caballeros 35; 963 913 317; open 10:30am–7:30pm Tue–Fri, 10:30am–6:30pm Sat, 1–8pm Sun; adm €7; www.sannicolas valencia.com

Torres de Serranos: Plaza de los Fueros; open 10am–7pm Tue–Sat, 10am–2pm Sun; adm €2, free Sun

Museo del Corpus: c/de Roteros 8; 963 153 156; open 10am–2pm & 3–7pm Tue–Sat, 10am–2pm Sun

Centro del Carmen: c/Museo 2; open 11am–7pm Tue–Sun; www. consorcimuseus.gva.es

IVAM: c/Guillem de Castro 118; open 10am–7pm Tue–Sun (to 8pm Fri); adm €5; www.ivam.es

■ Stop for delicious tapas at La Pilareta *(p84).*

TOP10 ⭐ La Catedral

Work first began on the Metropolitan Cathedral–Basilica of the Assumption of Our Lady of Valencia, to give it its full title, in 1262. There had been a spiritual centre here for more than 1,000 years before that: a Roman temple, a Visigoth cathedral and the original mosque of what was then Arabic Balansiya all once stood on this site. Spanning a variety of architectural styles, the cathedral is home to some superb frescoes – among the finest examples of the first Spanish Renaissance – and, allegedly, the Holy Grail itself.

① Puerta de los Apóstoles

Exiting onto Plaza de la Virgen, the Gothic Puerta de los Apóstoles once served as the entrance to the mosque that preceded the cathedral. The statues that surround it are copies of originals in the cathedral museum.

② The High Altarpiece

Painted in the early 16th century by Hernando de los Llanos, the altarpiece (right) was designed as a decoy – the panels hid a silver Renaissance altarpiece, melted down for coins during the Peninsular War.

③ El Miguelete

The landmark El Miguelete towers 51 m (167 ft) over Plaza de la Reina. The climb up the belfry's 207 steps is well worth the effort for the views across Valencia's Centro Histórico.

④ Puerta del Palau

This Romanesque door has seven concentric arches decorated with biblical scenes. Also known as Puerta de la Almoina, it was where the poor received alms.

⑤ The Renaissance Frescoes

The magnificent frescoes that decorate the ceiling of the apse (left) were only uncovered during repair works to the High Altarpiece in 2004. Painted by Italian artists Paolo da San Leocadio and Francesco Pagano da Neapoli in the late 15th century, they had remained hidden under the Gothic dome for more than 300 years. They depict 12 angel musicians surrounding the Virgin Mary.

6 Museo Catedral

The museum contains religious art and artifacts. A highlight is a huge processional monstrance, encrusted with precious stones **(left)**.

7 La Virgen del Coro

The 15th-century statue of the Virgin of the Chair (after her gold-decorated throne) is often surrounded by offerings from expectant mothers.

8 The Chapels

The cathedral has 24 chapels, containing among them assorted masterpieces including the remains of various saints and, if legend is to be believed, the Holy Grail *(see p17)*.

9 Puerta de los Hierros

The main entry **(right)** to the cathedral, the Baroque iron door, was designed by German architect Konrad Rudolf in 1703 and completed in 1741. The statues flanking the door are of St Peter Pascual on the right and St Thomas of Villanueva on the left.

THE LUCK OF LA VIRGEN

The pregnant women you may see doing laps of the cathedral are continuing a 19th-century tradition. They come here to pray to the statue of La Virgen del Coro and to circuit the interior nine times, once for each month of pregnancy, in the hope of a successful birth.

10 The Dome

A brilliant piece of Gothic architecture, the octagonal lantern tower uses a minimal stone frame, allowing for larger windows that flood the crossing below with light.

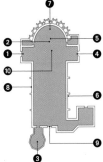

Floorplan of La Catedral

NEED TO KNOW

MAP M2 ■ Plaza de la Reina ■ www.catedralde valencia.es

Cathedral and Museo Catedral: open Mar–Jun & Oct–Nov: 10:30am–6:30pm Mon–Fri (to 5:30pm Sat), 2:30–5:30pm Sun; Jul–Sep: 10:30am–6:30pm Mon–Sat (from 2:30pm Sun); Dec-Feb: 10:30am–6:30pm Mon–Fri (to 5:30pm Sat); last adm: 1 hr before closing; adm €9 (incl. adm for Museo Catedral), concessions €6

El Miguelete: open Apr–Oct: 10am–7:30pm daily; Nov–Mar: 10am–6:30pm Mon–Fri, 10am–7pm Sat, 10am–1pm & 5:30–7pm Sun; adm €2.50

■ For a delicious light meal, head to Colmado LaLola *(see p84)*, just across from the main entrance to the cathedral.

■ Time a visit with the Tribunal de las Aguas *(see p71)*, held weekly by the Puerta de los Apóstoles.

Key Chapels in La Catedral

1 Capilla de San Sebastian

The powerful oil painting by Pedro de Orrente (1580–1645) in the Neo-Classical Chapel of St Sebastian, showing the saint's martyrdom, is recognized by many as one of the finest works in the cathedral.

2 Capilla del Santo Cáliz

The 15th-century Flamboyant Gothic altarpiece in this beautiful chapel holds at its centre the Alexandrian Cup, a polished red agate cup from the 1st century BCE that is reputedly the Holy Grail.

3 Capilla de San Francisco de Borja

This chapel's astonishing *St Francis Borgia at the Deathbed of a Dying Impenitent*, painted by Francisco Goya (1746–1828) in 1788, marks the first appearance of the super-natural in the artist's work.

4 Capilla de San Miguel Arcángel

Originally painted as a fresco by Paolo da San Leocadio (1447–1520) and Francesco Pagano (1471–1506), *The Adoration of the Shepherds* in

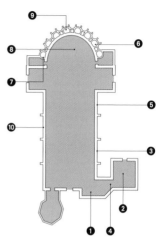

Floorplan showing the key chapels

the Chapel of St Michael the Archangel is thought to be the oldest Renaissance painting in existence in Spain.

5 Capilla de Santo Tomás de Villanueva

The reliquary bust that dominates the central altar here contains the skull and bones of St Thomas, a former archbishop of Valencia.

6 Capilla de la Virgen del Puig

This chapel is dedicated to Our Lady of El Puig. King James I of Aragon believed that the Marian image granted his troops victory in the Battle of El Puig in 1237 and in the subsequent Reconquest of Valencia.

7 Capilla de San Dionisio y Santa Margarita

The central panel of the altarpiece here portrays the two martyrs after whom the chapel is named, St Denis and St Margaret. Among the scenes of the Passion, the placement of the *Burial of Jesus* in the centre (rather than at the end) of the predella below is a Valencian tradition.

Capilla de San Miguel Arcángel

8 Capilla de San Jorge

Dominated by the painting of *St George at the Battle of the Puig*, this is where James I is said to have taken Mass after recapturing the city.

9 Capilla de San Vicente Ferrer

The altarpiece, images, oil paintings and canvases in this chapel all depict moments in the life of St Vincent Ferrer, who is the patron saint of the Autonomous Region of Valencia.

10 Capilla de la Resurección

Also known as the Corveta (Little Cave), this chapel takes its

Capilla de la Resurreción

name from the 16th-century translucent alabaster relief of the resurrection, although it is just as notable for containing the withered right arm of San Vicente Mártir.

HOW THE HOLY GRAIL CAME TO VALENCIA

There are hundreds of claimants to the Holy Grail, the cup that Jesus Christ drank from at the Last Supper, but only the chalice here in Valencia's cathedral has been recognized by the Vatican. Legend has it that after the death of the Virgin Mary, St Peter transported the Grail to Rome, where it remained until the 3rd century. Fearful for its safety during Emperor Valerian's persecution of Christians, Pope Sixtus II (himself executed in 258 CE) ordered the Grail to be taken to Huesca in northeastern Spain, where it stayed for the next 500 years. Christians fleeing the 8th-century Moorish invasion carried it up into the Pyrenees and then to the Royal Monastery of San Juan de la Peña. After spells at the Aljafería Palace in Zaragoza and the Real de Valencia, the Grail was finally given by Alfonso the Magnanimous to the cathedral in 1437.

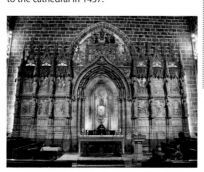

TOP 10 OTHER SITES RUMOURED TO HARBOUR THE HOLY GRAIL

1 Chalice Well, Glastonbury Tor, England, UK

2 Cattedrale di San Lorenzo, Genoa, Italy

3 Basilica of St Isidore, León, Spain

4 Dome of the Rock, Jerusalem, Israel

5 Montserrat, Spain

6 Rosslyn Chapel, Roslin, Scotland, UK

7 Château de Montségur, France

8 The Money Pit, Oak Island, Nova Scotia, Canada

9 Accokeek, Maryland, USA

10 Fort Knox, Kentucky, USA

The Holy Grail is at the centre of the Flamboyant Gothic altarpiece in the Capilla del Santo Cáliz.

TOP 10 ★ Mercado Central

One of the largest and most beautiful covered markets in Europe, the Mercado Central occupies a superb Modernista building in the heart of the Centro Histórico. Built to replace the street market that had grown up around the Convento de las Magdalenas, it was inaugurated in 1928. Despite its prominent location, it is very much a local market and is always full of Valencianos shopping for quality hams and cheeses, fruit and vegetables from La Huerta, and seafood fresh from the Mediterranean.

1 Modernista Details

With its tiled domes, vaulted wrought-iron beams, stained-glass windows and floral ceramics, the building is a defining example of early 20th-century Modernista architecture.

2 The Main Dome

The skylights, large windows, and octagonal iron cupola of the main dome allow plenty of light into the market (below). The dome sits on lattice beams to help support its weight.

The stained-glass exterior of the Mercado Central

4 La Cotorra del Mercat

The weather vane that perches 50 m (165 ft) above the main dome is known as La Cotorra del Mercat (The Parrot of the Market). The name is a reference to the chatter and bustle historically associated with the market stallholders – *cotorra* also means "chatterbox" in Spanish.

3 Central Bar

Ricard Camarena's Central Bar (see p84) is a great place to take a break. Pull up a stool and order a drink and some tapas or a *bocadillo* (sandwich) while watching the market ebb and flow.

NEED TO KNOW

MAP L3 ■ Plaza del Mercado ■ www.mercado centralvalencia.es

Open 7:30am–3pm Mon–Sat (no fish stalls on Mon)

■ Snack bars outside the market, in Plaza del Mercado, sell *churros* (fried doughnut sticks) for a snack on the go.

■ The market is at its most active first thing, when the stalls are at their fullest.

7 Meats
The quality of dried meats is exceptional, although the best cuts of jamón serrano are more expensive here than you will find elsewhere. The butchers' section is not for the faint-hearted, with sheep's heads, pigs' feet and ox tongues all on display **(left)**.

THE (EVENTUAL) CONSTRUCTION OF THE MERCADO CENTRAL

Plans were drawn up for a central market as early as 1882, but work was never started. In 1910, a competition to design the new building was won by the Catalan architects Francesc Guàrdia i Vial (1880–1940) and Alexandre Soler i Marc (1873–1949). King Alfonso XII laid the cornerstone in 1915, but due to a series of political and economic crises, the market was not fully completed for another 13 years.

10 The Fish Market Dome
Colourful fish pack the stalls of the large fish market. Looking up at the ceiling, visitors may notice that the dome here is topped by an interesting weather vane shaped like a swordfish in recognition of the produce on sale below it.

5 Spices
Cinnamon sticks, cloves, dried chillies, cardamom and all the essentials for a paella can be picked up at one of the spice stalls here. There is even a specialist saffron stall, La Casa del Azafrán.

8 Fish and Seafood
The *pescadería* (fish market) has its own section, on the right as you enter from Plaza del Mercado, with all sorts of fresh seafood piled high on ice. Look for *sépias* (cuttlefish), *erizos del mar* (sea urchins), *cigalas* (crayfish), *percebes* (goose barnacles) and huge pink langoustines.

6 Ceramics
The upper walls, roof supports and the inside of the main dome are all decorated with ceramic motifs – bunches of grapes and Valencian oranges, lemons and other fruit that represent the fertile gardens of La Huerta *(see p118)*.

9 Fruit and Vegetables
A quarter of the market's stalls have fresh fruit and vegetables **(right)**. Nearly 50 tonnes of fruit alone is sold here each day. Most produce is locally sourced and some stalls specialize in just one product, such as the beans used in paella and the spice saffron.

🔟 ⭐ La Lonja de la Seda

One of the finest civic buildings in Spain, La Lonja de la Seda (the Silk Exchange) is a masterpiece of Gothic architecture. Designed by Pere Compte and Joan Ibarra, it is a symbol of Valencia's power and wealth during the 15th and 16th centuries, when trading within these walls helped the city become one of Europe's most prominent economic centres. Work on the Sala de Contratación began in 1482, with the Consulado del Mar completed in 1548. La Lonja (Llotja in Valencian) was designated a UNESCO World Heritage Site in 1996.

1 Spiral Staircase

The magnificent spiral staircase that leads off the Sala de Contratacíon is an impressive feat of architectural engineering. Interestingly, the stone steps have no central axis and are supported only by the perimeter wall and the steps below.

2 Consulado del Mar

The Consulate of the Sea, which once housed the Trades Tribunal, has a splended coffered ceiling **(left)** and a beautiful Renaissance loggia, which overlooks the Plaza del Mercado.

3 West Entrance

The rich decoration on this doorway facing the Plaza del Mercado has scenes of witchcraft on the central mullion and vividly depicted sins of the flesh on the jamb. It is sited near where construction of La Lonja began – marked by a carving of the Valencian coat of arms.

4 Patio de los Naranjos

Take a breather under the orange trees in the tranquil courtyard **(below)**.

5 Sala Dorada

The beautiful coffered ceiling in the Sala Dorada (Golden Room), on the first floor of the Consulado del Mar, took Juan del Poyo eight years to complete. It is made up of more than 650 separate pieces slotted together with barely a nail in sight. The polychrome wood features signs of the zodiac, animals and many copies of the city's coat of arms **(below)**.

6 Capilla de la Inmaculada Concepcíon

The pretty Chapel of the Immaculate Conception forms a link between the Sala de Contratación and the Consulado del Mar. Its star-shaped ceiling is believed to be the work of Juan Graus, who was architect to Isabella and Ferdinand.

THE SILK TRADE IN VALENCIA

Silk was brought to Spain during the Arab invasion, and its production in Valencia rocketed when velvet weaving was introduced by artisans from Genoa, Italy in 1465. This led to the creation of a silk weavers' quarter – the Barrio de Velluters – and the foundation of the Colegio del Arte Mayor de la Seda *(see p88)*. By the end of the 17th century, Valencia had overtaken Toledo as the country's main producer of silk. It remained the city's principal industry until the advent of mass-produced fabrics in the 19th century.

7 Sala de Contratacíon

Trading of first silk and then commodities took place in the majestic Sala de Contratación (Hall of Commerce), La Lonja's most astonishing sight. Eight slender columns spiral up 12 m (39 ft) from the black marble floor, eventually merging into the elegant rib-vaulted ceiling **(above)**.

8 Tribunal del Comercio

The Consulado del Mar is split across two levels. The ground-floor hall once housed the Tribunal del Comercio (Trade Tribunal), an institution set up during the 13th century to handle matters of maritime trade.

9 Torreón

The crenellated central tower would not look out of place in a castle. Its upper two floors used to house a prison for merchants who failed to pay their debts or went bankrupt.

10 Gargoyles

Although normally associated with religious buildings, gargoyles **(right)** crown the exterior balustrades of the civic Silk Exchange; there are 28 in total, carved into the shapes of fantastical beasts, winged men and bats – the last being a symbol of the city.

NEED TO KNOW

MAP L3 ■ Calle de la Lonja
■ www.valencia.es

Open 10am–7pm Tue–Sat, 10am–2pm Sun; closed 1 & 6 Jan, 1 May, 25 Dec

Adm €2, concessions €1, under 7s free; free Sun

Audio guide €3

■ The Mercado Central *(see pp18–19)* is located directly opposite La Lonja so it's easy to pop over for a tapas lunch at the Central Bar after your visit here.

■ The audio guide provides the only on-site information and includes a wealth of detail on the exterior as well.

🔟 ⭐ Jardín del Turia

Valencianos are rightly proud of the Jardín del Turia, a magnificent stretch of gardens, shaded paths and cycling tracks following the former course of the Río Turia. After the Turia flooded in 1957, city authorities diverted its flow to the south of the city and invited urban planners and landscape artists to design different sections (known as *trames*) of a 9-km- (5.5-mile-) long municipal park. The dry riverbed was planted with orange trees and palms, and fountains and ponds were added. The gardens were finally opened in 1986.

1 Real Monasterio de la Santísima Trinidad

In the 15th century this monastic complex was the residence of Queen María of Castille, who is also buried here. It's now home to nuns and only the church is open for visitors.

2 Palau de la Música

Designed by architect José María de Paredes, the glass-domed concert hall has become a city landmark. It is home to the city's municipal orchestra (below).

Jardín del Turia with cycle tracks and footpaths

3 Parque de Cabecera

Leafy Cabecera gives a good idea of how the Río Turia would have once looked. Footpaths and boardwalks circumnavigate an artificial lake where visitors can rent pedalos.

4 Isla de las Esculturas

Fashioned from pieces of scrap iron, the works that make up artists Lucas Karrvaz and Antonio Marí's Island of Sculptures include a metal forger and a farmer and his dog.

5 Puente de la Trinidad

Built by Mateu Texidor between 1401 and 1407, stocky Puente de la Trinidad is the oldest bridge in the city. The Baroque statues halfway across depict Valencia-born saints (right).

6 Puente de las Flores

This bridge is a stunning sight, decorated with more than 10,000 colourful flowers – mostly cyclamen and geraniums – throughout the whole year.

7 Azud de Rovella

Badly damaged by the flood of 1957, this stone weir was used to divert water from the Río Turia into one of the eight *acequías* (irrigation channels) that feed the gardens of La Huerta (see p118).

Map of Jardín del Turia

9 Puente del Mar

The pedestrian Puente del Mar was built in 1596 by Francisco Figueroa to link the city with its port. Stone alcoves at the end of the bridge hold statues of San Pascual Bailón and the Virgin Mary.

8 Puente de la Exposición

Spanning the gardens above Alameda metro station, architect Santiago Calatrava's Modernist bridge was inaugurated in 1995 and is nicknamed La Peineta for its likeness to an ornamental comb.

10 Parque Gulliver

Lying prone as if he has just been washed up on the shores of Lilliput, this 70-m- (230-ft-) long figure **(above)** from Jonathan Swift's 1726 satirical novel *Gulliver's Travels* makes a unique playground for children. Gulliver's hair and clothes are sculpted into ramps and slides where children can play.

NEED TO KNOW

Map J1–P4

Real Monasterio de la Santísima Trinidad: c/Trinidad 13; 960 961 855; mass only; www. monasteriotrinidad.es

Palau de la Música: Paseo de la Alameda; 963 375 020; www. palauvalencia.com

Parque de Cabecera: Avda Pío Baroja; open 24 hrs

Parque Gulliver: open Mar & Oct: 10am–7pm daily; Apr–Jun & Sep: 10am–8pm daily; Jul & Aug: 10am–1:30pm & 5:30–9pm daily; Nov–Feb: 10am–5:30pm daily

■ Here you're never far from a tapas bar

or restaurant, with plenty of excellent options in the northern Centro Histórico and in Alameda and L'Eixample.

■ One of the best ways to explore the gardens is by bicycle. These can be rented from Valencia Bikes at Pg de la Pechina 32 *(650 621 436; www. valenciabikes.com)*.

Following pages L'Umbracle garden walkway, Ciudad de las Artes y las Ciencias

★ Ciudad de las Artes y las Ciencias

Innovative is an understatement for the dazzling City of Arts and Sciences, an ensemble of cutting-edge architecture that runs along a lush, attractively landscaped section of the Jardín del Turia. All bar one of these space-age buildings were designed by Valencian star architect Santiago Calatrava, who, in 1991, won the commission to regenerate a neglected area. The seven structures took 13 years to build and the project ran massively over budget, but the result is one of the most stunning architectural sights in Spain.

The futuristic buildings of the Ciudad de las Artes y las Ciencias

1 Palau de les Arts Reina Sofía
The spectacular opera house and performing arts centre has four venues that seat more than 3,000 people.

2 Pont de l'Assut de l'Or
This 125-m- (410-ft-) high suspension bridge takes its name from a dam that used to fjord the Río Turia near here.

3 Oceanogràfic
Designed by Félix Candela, this is Europe's largest aquarium. It is divided into a series of major climate zones representing different marine ecosystems.

4 Submarino
Oceanogràfic's flagship building is aesthetically shaped like a giant lily flower. It is the setting for an underwater restaurant **(below)**.

5 Museu de les Ciències
Calatrava regularly tries to work aspects of animal anatomy into his architecture – the structure of this interactive science museum resembles a whale skeleton. Its engaging and family-friendly exhibits cover subjects such as space **(above)** and the human body.

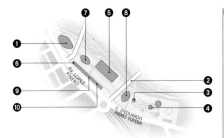

Map of Ciudad de las Artes y las Ciencias

7 Hemisfèric

Inaugurated in 1998, this planetarium and 3D IMAX cinema was the first of the complex's buildings to open to the public. Its shape mimics a huge eye, best seen when the "eyelids" are open and the building is reflected in the pool.

8 ÇaixaForum - Àgora

This exhibition space is designed to resemble a Venus flytrap. Major art exhibitions, talks, screenings, family activities and other cultural events are hosted here.

6 Mya

The City of Arts and Sciences has its own underground nightclub (see p97), accessed from L'Umbracle Terraza via a spiral staircase.

9 L'Umbracle Terraza

This bar is surrounded by the Umbracle's rich foliage and sits beneath its illuminated arches.

10 Umbracle

Built as a gateway to the whole complex, the Umbracle consists of 55 sunken arches that curve over a garden of tropical plants (below) and an open-air gallery.

NEED TO KNOW
MAP F6

Palau de les Arts Reina Sofía: Avda Professor López Piñero 1; guided tours 11am, 12:15pm & 1:30pm daily; €10.90, concessions €8.50; www.lesarts.com

Oceanogràfic: c/Eduardo Primo Yúfera 1; open Jan–mid-Jun & mid-Sep–Dec: 10am–6pm daily (to 8pm Sat); mid-Jun–mid-Jul & first two weeks in Sep: 10am–8pm daily; mid-Jul–

Aug: 10am–midnight daily; adm €30.70, concessions €22.90; www. oceanografic.org

Submarino: c/Eduardo Primo Yúfera 1; 662 860 595; closed D Sun

Museu de les Ciències: Avda Professor López Piñero 7; opening hours vary, check website; adm €8, concessions €6.20; www.cac.es

Hemisfèric: Avda Professor López Piñero 7; films daily

from 11am, book ahead; adm €8.70, concessions €6.70; www.cac.es

CaixaForum - Àgora: c/Eduardo Primo Yúfera 1A; 960 901 960; open 10am–8pm daily; adm €6, under 16s free

- Combined tickets to the buildings allow you to spread your visit over three consecutive days.

- The complex has several cafés and restaurants.

Key Features of Ciudad de las Artes y las Ciencias

Underwater tunnel in Oceanogràfic

two large murals. The CaixaForum, meanwhile, features blockbuster art exhibitions.

6 3D Screen, Hemisfèric
The Hemisfèric's IMAX dome features a vast concave digital 3D screen using a system that is around 360 times more powerful than an average home projector.

7 Calle Mayor, Museu de les Ciències
The science museum's exhibition space, the Calle Mayor, offers an excellent insight into the structural design of the building, the five giant columns here supporting its weight.

1 Oceans, Oceanogràfic
Two tanks holding marine life from the Atlantic and the Pacific oceans are connected by Europe's longest underwater tunnel.

2 Water
Water is a theme throughout the complex: the science museum resembles the bones of a whale, Oceanogràfic is an aquarium and pools surround several buildings.

3 Plants and Trees
The complex is set in a verdant stretch of the Jardín del Turia. Gardens of palm trees surround the opera house and about 6,000 plants line the Umbracle.

4 Tiles
In a nod to Valencia's long history of ceramic production, thousands of *trencadís* (broken mosaic tiles) were used to decorate the surfaces of the opera house, the walls of the promenade and some of the reflecting pools.

5 Artwork
The opera house is home to several art installations designed by Santiago Calatrava, including

8 Main Auditorium, Palau de les Arts Reina Sofía
The main venue's shell shape gives it exceptional acoustics. It is a great place to hear symphonic concerts.

Palau de les Arts Reina Sofía

9 Astronomy Garden, Umbracle
At the eastern end of the Umbracle, this garden contains a variety of astronomical instruments: a solar clock, a lunar clock and inventions that track the sun's distance from earth, the equinox cycle and the stars.

10 Temperate and Tropical, Oceanogràfic
Shaped like the hull of a boat, the beautifully designed Caribbean and Indo-Pacific Hall features hundreds of tropical triggerfish.

SANTIAGO CALATRAVA

Spanish architect Santiago Calatrava Valls

Born in Valencia in 1951, architect Santiago Calatrava is best known for creating sculptural bridges, ultra-modern railway stations and public buildings such as sports complexes, museums and cultural centres that display a blend of innovative engineering and elegant design. After graduating as an architect from the Polytechnic University of Valencia in 1974, he moved to Zurich, where he qualified as a civil engineer and set up his first architecture practice in 1981. Many of Calatrava's commissions are defined by his interest in biomorphic forms, evident in the Museu de les Ciències (which is shaped like a whale skeleton) and the Lyon-Saint Exupéry Airport Railway Station (a bird with spread wings) in France. Occasionally, Calatrava also introduces greater complexity to his works by adding moving parts – both Hemisfèric and the Museum of Art in Milwaukee, USA, include movable brise-soleil. While Calatrava is not without his critics, who point to structural issues with a number of his projects and a growing reputation for blowing his budgets, he is undeniably an architect like no other.

TOP 10 OTHER CALATRAVA DESIGNS

1 **Montjuïc Communications Tower**, *Barcelona (1992)*

2 **Oriente Station**, *Lisbon (1998)*

3 **Bodegas Ysios**, *La Rioja Alavesa (2001)*

4 **Turning Torso**, *Malmö (2001)*

5 **MAM**, *Milwaukee (2001)*

6 **Liege-Guillemins Station**, *Liege (2009)*

7 **Stazione Reggio Emilia AV Mediopadana**, *Reggio Emilia (2013)*

8 **Museu do Amanhã**, *Rio de Janeiro (2015)*

9 **World Trade Center Transportation Hub**, *New York (2016)*

10 **St Nicholas Greek Orthodox Church**, *New York (2022)*

The Museu de les Ciències is a typical example of Calatrava's interest in biomorphic architectural design.

🔟 ⭐ Museo de Bellas Artes

Set in the beautiful 17th-century Collegio Seminario de San Pío V, just across the Jardín del Turia from the Centro Histórico, the Museo de Bellas Artes was founded in 1837. One of the finest galleries in Spain, it houses an outstanding body of regional art. Highlights include the work of Primitive Valencian painters, a fine Renaissance collection that features pieces by Pintoricchio and El Greco, and over 40 paintings by Joaquín Sorolla, much of whose work was inspired by his observations of daily life on the beach at El Cabanyal.

Portrait of Joaquina Candado ①

One of half a dozen Francisco Goya (1746–1828) paintings in the museum, this portrait of his housekeeper **(right)** was painted in 1790 during a visit to Valencia. It is a skillful combination of landscape and portraiture.

② Equestrian Portrait of Don Francisco de Moncada

This portrait of Francisco de Moncada **(below)**, former Governor General of the Netherlands, shows why Anthony Van Dyck (1599–1641) became such a successful court painter – its composition expertly conveys the subject's importance and authority.

④ Self-Portrait

The only self-portrait painted by Diego Velázquez's (1599–1660), this was painted in Rome, when the artist was around 50 years of age. Its sombre austerity is believed to result from the Spaniard's reflections on growing old.

⑤ Altarpiece of Friar Bonifacio Ferrer

Commissioned by San Vicente Ferrer's brother, Gherardo Starnina's (1360–1413) altarpiece for the Charterhouse of Porta Coeli is one of the most elaborate Gothic altarpieces in the world.

③ St Francis of Assisi

Different in style from his more famous work *St Francis at Prayer* in Antwerp, Belgium, this painting by Spanish Baroque artist Bartolomé Esteban Murillo (1617–82) shows St Francis of Assisi experiencing his vision of Christ.

⑥ Virgin of the Fevers

Also known as *Madonna and Child with a Bishop*, this work **(left)** was painted by Italian artist Pintoricchio (1454–1511) on a commission by Francisco Borgia (seen kneeling on the right) for his appointment as the Bishop of Teano.

Triptych of the Insults (7)

This triptych **(right)** by Dutch artist Hieronymus Bosch (1450–1516) shows scenes from the Passion of Christ. The second figure on the left in the central panel is thought to be a self-portrait.

Floorplan of the Museo de Bellas Artes

- **1** Portrait of Joaquina Candado
- **2** Don Francisco de Moncada
- **3** St Francis of Assisi
- **10** Crucifixion
- **4** Self-Portrait
- **9** St Sebastian Attended by St Irene and Her Maid
- **8** St John the Baptist
- **6** Virgin of the Fevers
- **5** Altarpiece of Friar Bonifacio Ferrer
- **7** Triptych of the Insults

Key to Floorplan
- ■ Ground floor
- ■ First floor
- ■ Second floor

MUSEUM GUIDE

The museum's collection is organized in a rough chronological order: the main hall on the ground floor is filled with pieces of early Valencian art and architecture that span from the medieval period through to the Renaissance. The side galleries run from 15th-century Flemish painting to Romantic art. The collection of Joaquín Sorrolla's work is in the Edificio Perez Castiel, while the Gallery of Women Artists is on the second floor.

(8) St John the Baptist

This magnificent work by El Greco (1541–1614) reflects his strong links with Byzantine painting. The painting influenced many aspects of 19th-century Modernism.

(9) St Sebastian Attended by St Irene and Her Maid

One of the highlights of the museum, this is a powerful example of José de Ribera's (1591–1652) tenebrist style. The brightly illuminated figure of St Sebastian is contrasted against a background of almost complete darkness.

(10) Crucifixion

Best known for his still lifes, Antonio de Pereda y Salgado (1611–1678) also painted many religious pieces, including this 1660 representation of Jesus being crucified on Mount Calvary.

NEED TO KNOW

MAP N1 ■ c/San Pío V 9 ■ www.museobellas artesvalencia.gva.es

Open 10am–8pm Tue–Sun; closed 1 Jan & 25 Dec

Guided tours: Mon–Fri (book: 963 870 319)

■ There are plenty of tapas bars just across the road in the Jardín del Turia, including Taberna La Somorra (see p84).

■ Don't miss the Mariano Benlliure sculpture gallery; it is on the left of the entrance hall.

Works by Valencian Artists

① Valencian Rump

Joaquín Sorolla's colourful *Grupa Valanciana* (1906) – featuring his children, Joaquín and María, on horseback in traditional dress – is typical of his cheerful celebrations of Valencian identity.

② Preparations for the Crucifix

The impact of Caravaggio on Spanish artists is seen in the use of dark and light contrasts in this 1615 depiction of the Crucifixion by Juan Ribalta (c 1596–1628).

③ Apparition of Christ to St Ignatius de Loyola

Jerónimo Jacinto de Espinosa (1600–1667) was a prolific ecclesi-astical painter, and the golden light surrounding the dove (symbolizing the Holy Spirit) in this important altar painting from 1631 is a good example of his pious aesthetic.

④ Annunciation

A monumental diptych by local artist Jaume Baçó (c 1411–1461), known as Jacomart, this work depicts the Archangel Gabriel (kneeling, on the left) and the

***Annunciation* by Jacomart**

Virgin of the Annunciation in a style heavily influenced by Flemish Primitive painting.

⑤ The Parents of Mariano Benlliure

This affectionate plaster cast of Angela Gil and Juan Benlliure Tomás was sculpted by Mariano Benlliure (1862–1947) in 1915. It is a copy of a bronze cast that the artist originally made for their grave in the cemetery in El Cabanyal *(see p46)*.

⑥ Portrait of Captain General Ramón María de Narváez

Vicente López Portaña's (1772–1850) last painting shows Spanish conquis-tador Narváez at the June 1849 signing of the Amnesty Decree for prisoners of the Carlist uprising.

⑦ Predella with Five Scenes of the Passion of Christ

This predella by Joan Reixach (1411–86) formed part of an altarpiece in La Cartuja de Vall de Crist, a Carthusian monastery in Altura.

⑧ Seascape

A gift to his friend Pedro Gil, this painting of fishermen dragging

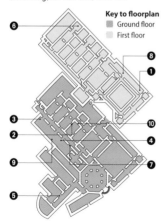

Key to floorplan
- ▨ Ground floor
- ▨ First floor

Floorplan of the Museo de Bellas Artes

a boat ashore (1907) by Joaquín Sorolla captures the artist's ardent brushstrokes and the importance of light and shadow in his work.

9 Altarpiece of the Immaculate Conception

Commissioned by the abbess of the Convento de la Puridad, this altarpiece was painted in 1515 by Nicolau Falcó (c 1470–1527).

10 The Mystical Wedding of the Venerable Agnesio

The Spanish Renaissance artist Joan de Joanes (1510–1579) painted this panel in memory of Valencian poet, preacher and philosopher Juan Bautista Jerónimo Agnesio, who can be seen on the left, placing a wedding ring on the finger of St Agnes.

The Mystical Wedding of the Venerable Agnesio by Joan de Joanes

JOAQUÍN SOROLLA: THE MASTER OF LIGHT

Born in Valencia in 1863, Joaquín Sorolla y Bastida is credited with the birth of modern painting in Spain. Although he also painted portraits and serious social works, Sorolla is best known for the iridescent beach scenes that so vividly portrayed everyday Valencian life. The emphasis he placed on expressive brushstrokes gave his canvases a rich textural depth, but it was the exquisite way that he managed to capture the fleeting effects of the Mediterranean sun, in sharp whites and shady blues, that earned him the moniker the "master of light". It was only during the painting of *La Vuelta de la Pesca (The Return from Fishing)* in 1894, now on display in the Musée d'Orsay in Paris, that Sorolla settled on his style. Inspired by fishermen on the beach at El Cabanyal, the painting marked a shift away from his previous adherence to subject matter, and from then on, he focused entirely on his own interpretation of light and shadow.

TOP 10 EVENTS IN THE LIFE OF JOAQUÍN SOROLLA

1 Born in Valencia (27 February 1863)

2 Orphaned when both parents die of cholera (1865)

3 Enrols in the Real Academia de Bellas Artes de San Carlos (1879)

4 Moves to Rome to study painting at the Spanish Royal Academy (1885)

5 Marries Clotilde Garcia del Castillo (1888)

6 Moves to Madrid (1890)

7 Wins the Grand Prix for *Sad Inheritance* (1900)

8 Appointed Officer of the Legion of Honour (1906)

9 Suffers a stroke (1920)

10 Dies in Madrid (10 August 1923)

La Vuelta de la Pesca by Joaquín Sorolla enjoyed great success at the Paris Salon and paved the direction of his mature style.

🔟 ⭐ Las Fallas

One of the most riotous festivals in Spain, Las Fallas celebrates the arrival of spring with a week-long party crackling with fireworks, parades and bonfires. The festival dates back more than 250 years and is focused around the elaborate monuments, or *fallas* (*falles* in Valencian), that are set alight on St Joseph's Day (19 March). Fashioned from papier-mâché and polystyrene, *fallas* are made up of cartoonish figurines known as *ninots*. Each neighbourhood has its own committee in charge of setting up their *falla*.

5 Cavalcada del Patrimoni

This parade, held on 10 March, leads from La Lonja to the Plaza del Ayuntamiento. Added to the UNESCO list of Intangible Cultural Heritage in 2016, the parade highlights different aspects of Valencian culture.

1 La Mescletà

A cacophonous pyrotechnic display, La Mescletà is held at 2pm daily from 1 March on Plaza del Ayuntamiento, with the final one on 19 March, which is always the most deafening of the lot. The Mescletàs gradually increase in volume until their dramatic finale, known as the *Terratrèmol* (Earthquake).

2 La Crida

Las Fallas officially begins on 24 February with *La Crida* (the Call), when the Fallas Queen opens it with a sound-and-light show and fireworks at the Torres de Serranos **(above)**.

3 La Iluminación

Several of the committees in Ruzafa and La Malvarossa districts create elaborate installations made from thousands of light bulbs. Among the most spectacular are those in Calle de Cuba in Ruzafa.

6 Ninot Exhibition

Held in the Museu de les Ciències *(see p26)* from 5 February to 15 March, this display features about 800 *ninots*, the best from each *fallas* committee. The *ninot* that receives the most votes each year from a public vote is saved from being destroyed by fire in the Indult del Foc.

4 Ofrena de Flors

Dressed in traditional attire **(right)**, *falleras* (the women of the *fallas* committees) descend on the Plaza de la Virgen on 17 and 18 March to offer flowers to the Virgen de los Desamparados.

NEED TO KNOW

www.visitvalencia.com, www.fallas.com

■ *Buñuelos*, deep-fried dough balls, are the usual snack of Las Fallas.

■ Most of the *fallas* are set up in the Centro Histórico or around Ruzafa and L'Eixample, where they also tend to be the most impressive.

9 La Plantà

La Plantà marks the moment when the *fallas* are put in place **(left)**; artists work through the night to meet the 8am deadline on 16 March. If a *falla* is not finished on time it is disqualified from the competition that judges which neighbourhood has created the best *falla*.

7 La Cremà

A week of lively festivities culminates on the night of 19 March with La Cremà, when Valencia is lit up with the flames of burning *fallas*. The huge main *falla* on Plaza del Ayuntamiento is always the last one to be condemned to flames.

8 Nit del Foc

Several nights of fireworks displays in the Jardín del Turia *(see pp22–3)* culminate at midnight on 18 March. The impressive *Nit del Foc* (Night of Fire) sees many thousands of rockets taking off over the dry riverbed at Alameda.

Map of the locations of key Fallas events

10 Cavalcada del Foc

Spectators can expect plenty of fireworks at this colourful, noisy parade **(above)**, which sets off from Plaza Puerto del Mar at 7pm on 19 March, the final night.

🔟⭐ Parque Natural de la Albufera

Less than 10 km (6 miles) south of the city, the extensive wetlands of the Parque Natural de la Albufera are some of the most important ecological areas in Europe. As well as the vast freshwater lake that gives the park its name – *al-buhaira* means "the lake" in Arabic – visitors can enjoy the beautiful blend of marshes, lagoons, rice fields, coastal forests, sand dunes and beaches. Several excellent nature trails crisscross the dunes that separate the lake from the sea, and scenic cycle paths connect most of the main sights.

1 Muntanyeta dels Sants

One of the highest points in La Albufera, topped by a 17th-century hermitage, Muntanyeta dels Sants is the best place to appreciate the park's patchwork of rice fields.

2 Ullal de Baldoví

One of the park's few remaining freshwater springs, this tiny reserve is a haven for birds and also harbours vulnerable local wildlife, such as the European pond turtle.

NEED TO KNOW

Map B5

Centro de Interpretación Racó de l'Olla: Carretera del Palmar; open 9am–2pm daily; www.parques naturales.gva.es

▪ Lunch at one of the paella restaurants in El Palmar is a must.

▪ Take a boat trip at sunset with Paseos en Barca por la Albufera (www.paseoenbarca albufera.com) or in a traditional *albuferenc* with Natura Albufera (www.albuferapaseo senbarca.com).

3 La Albufera

The huge lake (above) in the middle of the wetlands is the same size as the city of Valencia but less than a metre deep on average. It was formed 6,000 years ago when sediments accumulating at the mouths of the Túria and Júcar rivers eventually joined. It is now connected to the sea by a series of canals, known as *golas*.

Map of Parque Natural de la Albufera

4 Puerto Catarroja

This old Roman port is a reliable place to see the traditional wooden boats (known as *albuferencs*) that still ply the channels around the lake. This is also the traditional home of *all i pebre*, the Valencian dish of spicy stewed eels and potatoes.

6 El Palmar

Dozens of rice restaurants line the sun-baked streets of El Palmar **(left)**, a fishing village that is the birthplace of paella.

7 Beaches

More than a dozen beaches run along the coast between Pinedo in the north near the city and the Gola de Sant Llorenç, at the park's southern boundary. They range from ever-popular places like the vast Playa de El Saler to remote stretches that can only be accessed on foot.

BIRDLIFE IN LA ALBUFERA

La Albufera's diverse habitats harbour more than 350 species of birds, including flamingos, black-crowned night heron, the rare purple gallinule and birds of prey such as the booted eagle and the Western marsh harrier. The park's lagoons and marshes provide a vital refuge on the journey between Africa and the Arctic, and numbers can swell to more than 50,000 birds during the annual migratory months.

8 La Devesa

The forested sandbar separating the lake from the sea is known as La Devesa **(right)**. This fragile ecosystem of dunes runs for 30 km (19 miles) along the coast and is mostly made up of palms, pines and dense Mediterranean scrub.

5 El Saler

This easy-going Albuferan village takes its name from the triangular thatched fishing huts *(barracas)* that were used to store salt here before it was transported north to Valencia, though most have been destroyed. This is a good base for walks along the beach.

9 Centro de Interpretación Racó de l'Olla

Set in its own nature reserve, this visitor centre is an excellent place for visitors to familiarize themselves with the local fauna and flora – there is an observation tower and several hides **(below)** overlooking a lagoon that is often full of flamingos.

10 Tancats

The rice fields that give the marshes their patchwork quality are known as *tancats* in Valencian. Reclaimed from the lake during the 18th and 19th centuries, these plots of land were enclosed with dykes so that water levels could be regulated throughout the rice-growing cycle.

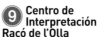

𝗧𝗢𝗣 10 ⭐ Xàtiva

The pretty town of Xàtiva (Jativa) is best-known for the Castillo de Xàtiva, a lofty castle fortified by both the Romans and the Carthaginians. It occupied a strategic location on the ancient Via Augusta that stretched back across the Pyrenees to Rome and down through Spain to the port of Cádiz. Several chapels line the road up to the castle, and the narrow streets of Xàtiva's Old Town itself have handsome churches and museums. Plaza del Mercado converts into a busy market on Tuesdays and Fridays.

2 Hospital Real

Founded in 1244 by Jaume I, the 16th-century Royal Hospital features an interesting mix of Gothic and Renaissance styles on its façade **(left)**. Most endearing are the angels that are playing musical instruments along the canopy arch of the main doorway.

4 Torre de Santa Fe

Sitting at the castle's highest point, the original Torre de Santa Fe was destroyed by a strong earthquake in 1813. The round tower that was built to replace it now offers fine views over Xàtiva below and the rolling hills beyond.

1 Capilla de la Reina María

Jaume II, the Count of Urgell, is one of several prisoners who are buried in this Gothic chapel, rebuilt in the mid-1400s.

3 Puerta de Hierro

At the top of a winding road (Carreterra del Castillo), the Puerta de Hierro or Porta Ferrissa (Iron Door) is the entrance to the castle. The frieze seen above the door displays the town's coat of arms.

5 Prison of the Count of Urgell

Believing he should have been next in line for the throne, Jaume II, the Count of Urgell, staged an unsuccessful uprising against Ferdinand I and was imprisoned in this castle cell for 20 years until his death in 1434. His cell lies deep in the Castell Major **(below)**.

6 Colegiata Basílica de Santa María
The local saying "this takes longer than the work on the cathedral" refers to this grand church, also known as La Seu **(above)**, which remains unfinished, despite the fact that its construction began in 1596. Its museum of religious art includes a Gothic gold chalice donated by Pope Calixtus III.

7 Plaza de la Trinitat
This square sits at the heart of Xàtiva's medieval Old Town and is home to a lovely Gothic fountain, one of the last examples left untouched in Spain.

8 Castell Menor
The Lower Castle is the oldest part, dating way back to pre-Roman and Roman times. The Carthaginian general Hannibal Barca allegedly plotted the siege of Sagunto from here in the 3rd century BCE. From the site's elevated position, there are splendid views over the valley of Bixquert.

9 Museo de l'Almudí
Occupying a restored granary house, this archaeology museum **(right)** contains remains from Iberian, Visigothic and Roman rule, plus a beautifully carved Islamic water trough from the 11th century.

10 Iglesia de San Felix
One of the oldest churches in the Autonomous Region of Valencia, San Felix (Sant Feliú) was built in 1265. It houses a fabulous Gothic altarpiece as well as some weathered but impressive medieval murals from the 1300s.

THE BORGIAS IN XÀTIVA
One of the most powerful noble clans of the Renaissance, the scheming Borgia family (Borja in Spanish) produced two popes, both of whom were born in Xàtiva: Pope Calixtus III (1455–1458) and his nephew Pope Alexander VI (1492–1503), who was born in the Old Town.

NEED TO KNOW

Map B6

Castillo de Xàtiva:
Subida al Castillo; open 10am–9pm Tue–Sun; adm €6, concessions €4, under 8s free

Colegiata Basílica de Santa María: Plaza Calixto III; open 10:30am–1pm daily (from 11:30am Sun & public hols); adm €3

Iglesia de San Felix:
Carretera del Castillo; open 10am–1pm & 4– 7pm Mon–Sat (3–6pm in winter), 10am–1pm Sun

■ Enjoy great tapas at El Túnel (see p121).

■ To save yourself from the stiff climb up to the castle, catch a tourist train from the tourist office (12:30pm & 4:30pm; returns 1 hour later; €4.20).

C. MONCADA

PLAZA DEL MERCADO
C. DE LA CORREGERIA

CALLE MENOR
CUESTA

Castillo de Xàtiva

Map of Xàtiva

The Top 10 of Everything

Traditional dancing during Fiesta de la Virgen de los Desamparados

Moments in History

① Birth of a Roman City
Valentia Edetanorum was founded in 138 BCE by Roman legionnaires on what was then an island in the middle of the River Tyrus (Turia). The settlement was destroyed by Pompey in 75 BCE but rebuilt 50 years later by Emperor Augustus, who created a grand central forum under what is now Plaza de la Virgen.

② Christians and Visigoths
As the Roman Empire declined throughout the 5th century CE, the city's emergent Christian community grew steadily in power until it eventually took over the running of the Senate. Valentia came under the control of the Visigoths in the mid-6th century; although they built palaces and a cathedral, their rule was marked by economic strife.

③ Moorish Rule
In 714 CE, Muslim invaders from North Africa overthrew the Goths, introducing their language and religion to what they called Balansiya. With the break up of the Caliphate of Córdoba in 1010, Balansiya became the capital of its own *taifa*, or kingdom. El Cid briefly occupied the city at the end of the 11th century, and Jaume I captured it in 1238.

El Cid invading Valencia in 1094

④ Blossoming of the Arts
Following a tumultuous period of riots and wars, the 15th century was peaceful and highly prosperous. Buoyed by the trading of silk and other commodities, the city became one of the richest and most influential in Europe, enjoying a flourishing of culture and the arts.

⑤ End of a Kingdom
Valencia's decision to side with Charles VI, the Holy Roman Emperor, against Philip V during the War of the Spanish Succession heralded its end as an independent kingdom. Following Charles's defeat at the Battle of Almansa in 1707, Philip exacted revenge by repealing the city's privileges – devised by Jaume I over 450 years earlier – as part of a wider move to form a unified Spain.

Peninsular War events, Valencia

⑥ French Occupation
The Peninsular War (1807–14) between the Napoleonic Empire and Bourbon Spain – the latter aided by Britain and Portugal – saw the French briefly occupy Valencia between 1812 and 1813 under Marshall Louis-Gabriel Suchet.

⑦ A Time of Growth
Industrialization during the 1800s sparked a rapid expansion, as Valencia's population quadrupled over the course of the century and the city walls were torn down to make way for new housing and transport infrastructure.

The Spanish Civil War in 1936

8 Civil War

As the country became more divided between Left and Right, a revolt against the Second Spanish Republic led by General Francisco Franco in July 1936 marked the start of the Spanish Civil War. The Republican government moved its capital to Valencia in November 1936, but the city fell to Franco's Nationalist forces on 30 March 1939.

9 Life after Franco

Valencia suffered greatly along with the rest of Spain under General Franco's repressive rule, its economic hardships worsened by the flooding of the Río Turia in 1957, when more than 80 people died. Spain's return to democracy after the dictator's death in 1975 resulted in greater regional power. In 1983, the city became the autonomous Comunidad Valenciana, and the Valencian language was once again taught in schools.

10 Regeneration

Valencia's contemporary history has been marked by reinvention and regeneration. The building of the City of Arts and Sciences put Valencia on the map as a tourist destination, while the hosting of the America's Cup in 2007 overhauled the port area. In 2022 the city was selected as the World Design Capital, cementing its reputation as a champion of creativity.

TOP 10 HISTORICAL FIGURES

1 Decimus Junius Brutus Callaicus (180 BCE–113 BCE)
Brutus was a military commander and Consul of the Roman Republic in 138 BCE, the year he founded Valentia.

2 San Vicente Mártir (d 304 CE)
This priest, a patron saint of Valencia, was martyred by the Romans under Emperor Diocletian.

3 El Cid (1043–99)
Rodrigo Diaz de Vivar, a charismatic knight who ruled Valencia for five years, was known as the Lord.

4 Jaume I (1208–76)
A 13th-century warrior-king, Jaume I recaptured Valencia in 1238, forming the Aragonese kingdom of Valencia.

5 San Vicente Ferrer (1350–1419)
The patron saint of the Autonomous Region of Valencia, this Dominican friar was famous for his miracles.

6 Isabel de Villena (1430-90)
A writer and nun, De Villena's spiritual biography of Jesus, *Vita Cristi*, is considered a significant Valencian work.

7 Juan de Ribera (1532–1611)
Archbishop of Valencia, the influential Ribera was canonized in 1960.

8 Philip III (1578–1621)
His expulsion of the Moriscos (Moors who had converted to Christianity) damaged Valencia's economy.

9 Constanti Llombart (1843–93)
This writer and activist spearheaded La Renaixença, a movement focused on reviving Valencian as a language.

10 Rita Barbará (1948–2016)
Mayor of Valencia from 1991 to 2015, Barbará instigated an ambitious regeneration programme but her time in office was marred by corruption.

Former mayor, Rita Barbará

🔟 Places of Worship

1 Iglesia de San Juan de la Cruz

The austere façade of this Renaissance church (see p86) conceals an extravagant Rococo interior. Finely crafted by Hipólito Rovira and Luis Domingo in the 18th century, stucco angels, floral motifs and scenes from the Bible blanket the walls and ceiling in white and gold.

Tiles outside the Iglesia de San Juan de la Cruz

2 Iglesia de Santa Catalina

One of the oldest churches in Valencia, the Gothic Iglesia de Santa Catalina (see p80) is dedicated to St Catherine of Palma, a 16th-century nun who is Mallorca's only saint. Its distinctive hexagonal bell tower, an 18th-century Baroque addition, is one of the most recognizable landmarks in the Centro Histórico.

3 Basílica de la Virgen de los Desamparados

MAP M2 ■ Plaza de la Virgen
■ Open 7:30am–2pm & 4:30–9pm daily
■ www.basilicadesamparados.org

This pretty church is dedicated to one of the city's patron saints, Our Lady of the Forsaken. It has a venerated statue of the Virgin Mary, adorned with clothes and jewels. Nicknamed La Geperudeta, or the Little Hunchback, due to a curve in its back, the statue sits in an oval room whose dome is covered in frescoes by Antonio Palomino.

4 Parroquia de San Nicolás

The interior of this Gothic church (see p12) received a spectacular Baroque makeover at the end of the 17th century. Spanish artist Dionis Vidal spent three years painting the naves with scenes recounting the lives of St Nicolas and St Peter.

5 Iglesia de San Juan del Hospital

This church (see p78) was consecrated in 1238, making it the oldest in Valencia after the Reconquest. It originally housed a hospital, convent and cemetery. After falling into disrepair in the 1930s it was used as a cinema until Opus Dei took it over in the 1960s.

Mass in the Basílica de la Virgen de los Desamparados

Iglesia de los Santos Juanes

6 Iglesia de los Santos Juanes

Like many of Valencia's churches, the 1240 Iglesia de los Santos Juanes (see p80) was originally constructed on the site of an old mosque, although this incarnation dates from the 16th century. Statues of John the Baptist and John the Evangelist sit on its roof; the Baroque interior has a huge, fresco-coated dome.

7 Iglesia del Carmen

MAP L1 ■ Plaza del Carmen ■ Open 10am–7pm Tue–Sun

Consecrated in 1343, this parish church was once part of the monastery that now houses the Centro del Carmen (see p13). The Baroque renovation it received in the mid-17th century, with its scallop-shell niches and Solomonic columns, is best seen on the upper reaches of the façade that fronts Plaza del Carmen.

8 Real Colegio Seminario de Corpus Christi

This seminary college (see p88) is known as El Patriarca, after its founder, Juan de Ribera, Archbishop of Valencia and Patriarch of Antioch. It is a treasure trove of art: the church is covered in frescoes by the Genoese painter Bartolomé Matarana; the Chapel of the Monument's walls are decorated with Flemish tapestries; and the museum houses works by El Greco and Caravaggio.

9 Ermita de Santa Llúcia

MAP K4 ■ c/de l'Hospital 15 ■ Open 9am–1pm & 4–7pm Tue–Sat (to noon Sun)

This beautiful little hermitage, dedicated to the patron saint of the blind, was built by the Brotherhood of St Lucia in 1399. It was originally Gothic in style but now has a Baroque interior, with works of art that span several centuries.

10 Real Monasterío de Santa Maria del Puig

The Royal Monastery of Our Lady of El Puig (see p117) consists of two buildings: a Gothic church and a Renaissance-style monastery. It has also been used as a prison and a school, and today hosts government events, although it is still also home to monks from the Order of Our Lady of Mercy, founded in Barcelona in 1218 by St Peter Nolasco.

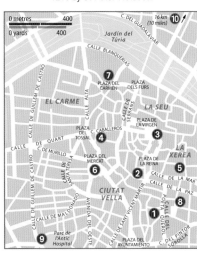

🔟 Architectural Highlights

The ornate exterior of Palacio del Marqués de Dos Aguas

1 Palacio del Marqués de Dos Aguas

The palace that houses the Museo Nacional de Cerámica *(see p88)* has the most lavish façade in Valencia, with a fantastically over-the-top Churrigueresque doorway designed by Hipólito Rovira and sculpted in alabaster by Ignacio Vergara.

2 Ciudad de las Artes y las Ciencias

The work of Santiago Calatrava and Felix Candela, these jaw-dropping Neo-Futurist designs *(see pp26–9)* culminate in the incredible Palau de les Arts Reina Sofía, which resembles an enormous cracked egg.

3 La Lonja de la Seda

This 16th-century temple of commerce is the city's definitive example of Gothic civil architecture *(see pp20–21)*. The superb Sala de Contratacíon rightly gets all the attention, but there are also some ingenious touches by stonemason Pere Compte, as well as doorways decorated with comical carvings.

4 Mercado Central

A huge fresh produce market and one of the most beautiful buildings in the city, the Mercado Central *(see pp18–19)* was designed in the Modernista style (the Spanish Art Nouveau) by Catalan architects Alexandre Soler i Marc and Francesc Guàrdia i Vial.

5 El Cabanyal
MAP G5

The old fishing quarter of El Cabanyal is awash with elegant townhouses whose entire façades have been covered in coloured tiles.

6 Estación del Norte

The main train station *(see p95)* was built between 1906 and 1917 by Valencian

Estación del Norte

architect Demetrio Ribes and features some lovely Modernista details, including original wooden ticket offices, ornamental lighting and stained-glass windows.

7 Mercado de Colón

The Mercado de Colón (see p96) was built in 1916 to serve the upper-class district of L'Eixample. It was designed by Francisco Mora, a pupil of the Catalan architect Doménech i Montaner, whose influence can be seen throughout.

8 Veles e Vents

Built for the 2007 America's Cup, this minimalist structure (see p110) was designed by David Chipperfield and Fermín Vázquez and took less than a year to build.

Veles e Vents in Valencia harbour

9 La Catedral

Valencia cathedral's interesting mishmash of contrasting styles is particularly evident in its three main entrances: the Baroque Puerto de los Hierros, the Gothic Puerta de los Apostoles and the Romanesque Puerta del Palau (see pp14–17).

10 Edificio de Correos y Telégrafos

There are post offices and then there is Valencia's monumental Edificio de Correos y Telégrafos (see p87). This Neo-Classical building was constructed between 1915 and 1922 by Zaragozan architect Miguel Ángel Navarro Pérez. Pop a postcard into one of the original lion's head postboxes and admire the beautiful stained-glass dome inside.

TOP 10 PLACES TO SEE CERAMIC TILES

Tiles in Horchatería de Santa Catalina

1 Horchatería de Santa Catalina
Sip on an ice-cold *horchata* while admiring the agricultural scenes on the walls of this historic café (see p84).

2 Mercado de Colón
Colourful tilework depicting farmers at work in La Huerta caps the façade of this Modernista masterpiece (see p94).

3 Casa del Oso
The iconic mosaic on this house (see p111) is the best of several spread around the El Cabanyal fishing quarter.

4 Salón de la Fama
This beautiful mosaic at the Museo y Colegio del Arte Mayor de la Seda (see p88) depicts an angel representing Valencian silk surrounded by the four continents known at the time.

5 Manises Tourist Office
The façade of this former pottery (see p117) is full of references to trade, productivity and quality manufacturing.

6 Museo de la Cerámica
Tiling in the Valencian kitchen on the second floor of this museum (see p88) shows historical functions and foods.

7 Consulado del Mar, La Lonja
The tile panels of Jaume I and San Vicente Ferrer at La Lonja (see p20) were made using the *socarrat* technique.

8 Estación del Norte
The old waiting room at this station (see p93) has beautiful mosaics depicting rural scenes from La Albufera.

9 Galería Dorada, Palau Ducal, Gandia
The mosaic at the Palau Ducal (see p118) reflects the four elements.

10 Palau de les Arts Reina Sofía
Broken mosaic tiles, known as *trencadís*, cover Santiago Calatrava's astonishing opera house (see p26).

🔟 Museums and Galleries

Valencian Gothic devotional art in the Museo de Bellas Artes

1 Museo de Bellas Artes

Valencia's Museum of Fine Arts (see pp30–31) is one of the most important galleries in Spain. It combines paintings by masters of the Renaissance with comprehensive collections of Valencian Gothic art and, in particular, works by the "master of light" Joaquín Sorolla.

2 Museo Nacional de Cerámica

Housed in a luxurious palace, this museum (see p88) is Spain's largest collection of ceramics, containing works spanning a range of styles, from Mudéjar bowls to pieces by Picasso. One of the highlights is the reconstruction of a typical Valencian kitchen, designed by the museum's founder, Manuel González Martí.

3 Centro del Carmen

The former monastery (see p13) that overlooks Plaza del Carmen hosts a variety of art exhibitions and events in the rooms that once served as the monks' dormitory and dining hall.

4 Museo y Colegio del Arte Mayor de la Seda

Valencia was designated the Western Capital of the Silk Route by UNESCO in 2016 (see p88), and this museum, set in a restored Gothic building in the old Barrio de Velluters, the silk weavers' district, is the best place to learn more about the history of the silk trade in the city.

5 Museo del Patriarca

Part of the Real Colegio Seminario de Corpus Christi, this small museum (see p88) forms part of the seminary's wider collection of fantastic art that was assembled by its founder, Juan de Ribera. It includes works by Jan Provost and Ignacio Pinazo.

6 Museo Fallero

Occupying a former convent near the Jardín del Turia, this museum (see p95) is home to every *ninot* that has survived Las Fallas. As well as seeing their evolution from wax to polystyrene, visitors can enjoy festival posters dating to 1929.

A *ninot* sculpture at the Museo Fallero

⑦ CaixaForum - Àgora

This striking space – part of the Ciudad de Arts y les Ciencies *(see pp26–7)* – hosts some of the city's biggest temporary art exhibitions. The centre isn't just focused on art however; musical performances and innovative talks are also held in the large auditorium.

⑧ La Almoina

All of the major eras of the city's past are featured at this superb archaeological museum *(see p77)*, with walkways running above and around Roman, Visigoth and Arabic remains, which include the foundations of a Visigoth cathedral (in the Chapel of St Vicente), Roman baths and the courtyard of a Moorish governor's house.

Institut Valencià d'Art Modern

⑨ Institut Valencià d'Art Modern (IVAM)

This highly regarded contemporary art museum *(see p13)* claims to have more than 10,000 works among its permanent collection, with everything from Abstract Expressionism to Pop Art. A sculpture garden was added to celebrate the museum's 30th anniversary in 2019.

⑩ Museu de les Ciències

"It is Prohibited Not to Touch" is the slogan of this hands-on museum in the City of Arts and Sciences *(see p26)*. Key exhibits include Talking Brains, where visitors can discover how language works; a conservation-minded look at the Mediterranean; and the great Forest of Chromosomes.

TOP 10 CULTURAL HEAVYWEIGHTS

Engraving of March reading a poem

1 Ausiàs March *(1400–59)*
One of the most influential poets of the 15th century.

2 Joanot Martorell *(c 1410–65)*
Knight-author of the chivalrous Valencian romance *Titant le Blanc*.

3 Pere Compte *(d 1506)*
Aragonese court architect and master stonemason whose designs include La Lonja de la Seda and Torres de Quart.

4 Joan Luis Vives *(1493–1540)*
Renaissance humanist known as the "father of modern psychology".

5 Joan de Joanes *(1507–79)*
Valencia's most important and influential Renaissance painter, also known as Vicente Juan Masip.

6 Hipólito Rovira *(1695–1765)*
The painter and sculptor behind the façade of the Palacio de Marqués del Dos Aguas, among others.

7 Teodoro Llorente Olivares *(1836–1911)*
A lawyer, writer and leading poet of La Renaixença, a cultural movement aimed at preserving Valencian language and identity.

8 Joaquín Sorolla *(1863–1923)*
Spain's most famous artist of the Impressionist movement.

9 Carmelina Sánchez-Cutillas *(1927–2009)*
Sánchez-Cutillas, an often overlooked poet and historian, wrote almost exclusively in Valencian.

10 Santiago Calatrava *(b 1951)*
A revolutionary architect known for his futuristic designs that can be seen in cities around the world.

🔟 Parks and Plazas

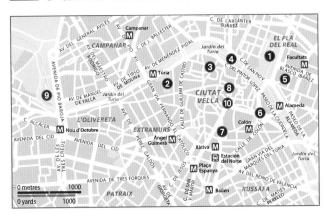

1 Jardines del Real

The former grounds of a royal palace, Valencia's largest gardens (see p104) are often used as a venue for the city's busy cultural calendar. Concerts are held here during July's Fería de Valencia and bookstalls line its pathways for the springtime Fería del Libro. The gardens are also known as Los Viveros.

Cacti in the Jardín Botánico

2 Jardín Botánico

The University of Valencia's botanical gardens (see p103) have occupied the orchards of the Huerto de Tramoyeres since 1802. Now a research centre, the gardens include 4,500 species of plants from around the world divided into collections that demonstrate their diversity, from fruit trees to medicinal plants.

3 Plaza del Carmen
MAP L1

This quiet, leafy plaza (see p45) in the northern reaches of the Centro Histórico is typical of the Old Town's hidden squares, with a few locals whiling away the afternoons under the shade of a gnarled old orange tree. The square is dominated by the 14th- century Iglesia del Carmen, the barrio's parish church.

4 Jardín del Turia

Much more than just a garden, the Jardín del Turia (see pp22-3) is a green lung for the city and an outdoor gym for its residents, with its series of tree-lined paths, cycle tracks and playing fields. Following the old course of the Río Turia, it runs for 9 km (6 miles) from Parque de Cabecera down to the City of Arts and Sciences.

5 Jardín de Monforte

These lovely gardens (see p106) were created by the Marqués de San Juan but are named after the family who took them over when he died in 1872. They are laid out in Neo-Classical style, with cypress hedges separating different sections that contain ponds, fountains, a summer pavilion and a wealth of fine statues sculpted in Carrara marble.

6 La Glorieta
MAP N3

Much changed since its foundation in 1812 by the French marshall Louis-Gabriel Suchet, this park is worth a visit for its enormous 165-year-old fig trees and the statues of notable Valencianos, including a bust of the painter Francisco Domingo Marqués by Mariano Benlliure. It also has a small park for children.

7 Plaza del Ayuntamiento
MAP L4

The main focus of the southern Centro Histórico, Plaza del Ayuntamiento *(see pp34–5)* is an attractive fountain-filled square. It is lined on two sides by the Neo-Classical Edificio de Correos y Telégrafos, Valencia's main post office, and the Town Hall that gives the square its name. Las Fallas reaches its finale with the burning of the main *falla* in the plaza.

8 Plaza de la Virgen

Visitors will probably keep returning to this central square *(see p77)*, the location of the cathedral and the pink Basílica de la Virgen de los Desamparados. The statues in the fountain represent the Río Turia and its eight main irrigation channels; representatives from the communities that formed around these channels meet here weekly at the Puerta de los Apóstoles.

Lake in the Parque de Cabecera

9 Parque de Cabecera

Focused around a gorgeous, twinkling lake, this landscaped park *(see p106)* at the northern end of the Jardín del Turia provides a natural transition between the Río Turia and its former course. Paths lead up to a hilltop viewpoint and along a riverside walkway through Mediterranean woodland. There is an open-air auditorium, boats to rent and a kids' play areas.

10 Plaza del Reina
MAP M3

More of a strung-out rectangle than a typical town square, this is one of the busiest plazas in Valencia, with honking traffic circulating around its flower-filled gardens. It is lined with palm trees and tall, elegant buildings whose ground floors are given over to cafés, tapas bars and gift shops. The cathedral sits at the plaza's northern end.

The Plaza de la Virgen with the fountain, cathedral and basilica

TOP 10 Beaches

Poolside at the Marina Beach Club

1 Playa de las Arenas

Las Arenas *(see p110)* attracts a slightly younger crowd than Valencia's other city beaches, drawn here by the swish Marina Beach Club. It is wide and clean, although the cranes in the nearby port provide a rather jarringly industrial back-drop. Spend a relaxed morning on the beach, then tuck into a lazy lunch of paella or *fideuà* (Valencian paella made with noodles) at a restaurant on the Paseo Marítimo.

2 Playa de la Malvarossa

Valencia's fantastic stretch of golden beaches are at their busiest around the ever-popular Playa de la Malvarossa *(see p111)* – the central section just north of the port – but the beach here still never gets that crowded. It is just a short tram ride from the city centre, and locals flock here year-round to sunbathe, socialize and play beach volleyball.

3 Playa de la Devesa
MAP B5

Set on the sand bar that runs for 30 km (19 miles) along the coast alongside the Parque Natural de la Albufera *(see pp36–7)*, this is a truly wild beach. Backed by lagoons and bordered by wildlife-filled canals, the beach and its rich ecosystem of coastal dunes can be explored on a variety of self-guided trails.

4 Playa de Pinedo
MAP B5

The beach at this traditional fishing village just outside the city has lovely honey-coloured sand and is backed by a long boardwalk with plenty of tapas bars and restaurants to choose from. It is easy to reach by bike, crossing the mouth of the diverted Río Turia along the way. There is a nudist area at the beach's southern end, beyond the boardwalk.

5 Playa de les Palmeres
MAP B5

Just under 30 km (19 miles) south of Valencia, on a slightly more built-up section of the Parque Natural de la Albufera coast, reliably windswept

Beachgoers at Playa de la Malvarossa

Kitesurfing on Playa de les Palmeres

Playa de les Palmeres is a popular spot with kitesurfers – a kitesurf school runs courses here in summer. Hop on one of the free municipal bikes and cycle along the town's promenade to enjoy the views.

6 Playa de El Saler

Located just behind the town of the same name, around 15 km (9 miles) south of Valencia, El Saler *(see p37)* is the best of several great beaches within the boundaries of Parque Natural de la Albufera. The fine white sands run for 2.5 km (2 miles) and are protected by a row of sand dunes and pine trees.

7 Playa de la Patacona

Bringing Valencia's 3-km- (2-mile-) long sweep of sand to an end, Playa de la Patacona *(see p110)* is a little bit harder to reach than the other city beaches to the south, but it is consequently much quieter, with just a smattering of locals whiling away the day at one of the area's *chiringuitos* (beach bars). This is the Alboroya neighbourhood beach, hence it is sometimes also known as Playa de la Aboroya.

8 Playa Port Saplaya
MAP B5

This purpose-built holiday village 7 km (4.5 miles) north of Valencia is known as Little Venice due to its colourful buildings and boat-lined marina. Its quiet beach has good facilities, including plenty of places to grab a cooling *horchata (see p65)* – the tiger nuts used in the drink are grown in the surrounding fields and were once shipped across Europe from the former port.

9 Playa de Gandía
MAP B6

This beach is wide enough that it never feels overcrowded, even during the summer, when it is "combed" by tractors to keep it pristine. Lines of palms and a sparkling promenade separate the beach from the road and the high rises behind, where there are plenty of restaurants and bars. Other facilities include playgrounds, basketball hoops and several beach volleyball nets.

10 Playa del Puerto de Sagunto
MAP B5

Popular with day-tripping Valencian families, this beach near the ancient town of Sagunto is well looked after and the sea is clean, despite its proximity to the town's port. Dunes back the beach to the south; its northern end is good for crabbing.

🔟 Sports and Activities

① Basketball

If there is a spare patch of wall in Valencia, chances are there will be a basketball hoop attached to it. But in order to see the real deal, head to the Fuente de Sant Lluis arena, also known as La Fonteta, in Na Rovella, just south of Ruzafa, which is home to the Valencia Basket Club. The team compete in the Liga ACB, which runs from October to May.

Basketball at Fuente de Sant Lluis

② Water Bikes

Open 11am–7:15pm daily

■ Adm

One of several watersports on offer in the main outdoor pool at the City of Arts and Sciences *(p30)*, these water bikes, available in ten-minute slots, are akin to a surfboard – with a handlebar attached. Paddle them by moving your feet in the same way you would on a step aerobics machine.

③ Pelota Valenciana

This uniquely Valencian sport is lightning fast and involves two teams batting a small ball (known as a *vaqueta*, made from wood and bull skin) over a net with their bare hands. There are several regional variants – the type of *pelota* favoured in Valencia is called Escala i corda. Dating from 1910, it is played on a four-walled court called a *trinquet*.

④ Football

It might well be a cliché, but football really is a religion in Spain. During the season (August to May), try to catch a game at La Mestalla, the magnificent home of Valencia CF, or at the smaller Estadi Ciutat de València, where the city's other major team, Levante UD, play their home matches. Both teams play in La Liga, Spain's top division.

⑤ Moto GP

The traditional finale to the Moto GP season is the Gran Premi de la Comunitat Valenciana. It is held at the Circuit Ricardo Tormo, 23 km (14 miles) to the west of Valencia, in November each year and is one of the biggest events in the motorcycle racing calendar, thanks in part to the large crowds the race draws.

⑥ Sailing

Valencia has a very strong sailing pedigree, having hosted the America's Cup twice (in 2007 and in 2010) as well as the annual Queen's Trophy Regatta, one of the most prestigious events in the country's sailing calendar. For the more casual sailor, sailing boats, catamarans and schooners can be chartered from a number of companies based in the Real Club Náutico.

Sailing off the coast of La Albufera

Cycling along Malvarrosa Beach

7 Cycling

Valencia is a superb city for cycling around, with nearly 150 km (93 miles) of cycle paths and a further 40 *ciclocalles*, streets where bikes are given the right of way. One of the best routes, particularly for families, runs through the Jardín del Turia. Lots of companies rent out bikes, and some allow customers to pick them up at one location and drop them off at another.

8 Diving

Diving Valencia: www.diving valencia.com

The marine life in Valencia's waters is surprisingly abundant, though the best dive sites are found further along the coast, such as Las Corvas, a couple of miles off Cullera, to the south, and the the Columbrete Islands to the north. Several companies offer beginners' lessons.

9 Rugby

Valencia has two professional teams who play in the lower leagues of Spanish rugby, but it is just as much fun watching the amateur games at the Camp de Rugby del Riu in the Jardín del Turia.

10 Hot-Air Ballooning

TotGlobo: www.totglobo.com

For a different perspective on the countryside around Valencia, take to the skies in a magical hot-air balloon ride. Morning flights take off from Bocairent, 35 km (22 miles) south of Xàtiva. Lasting around an hour, the flights involve drifting some 1,500 m (nearly 5,000 ft) above the ground.

TOP 10 SPORTING LEGENDS

1 Mundo (1916–78)
Valencia CF's Edmundo Suárez Trabanco, or "Mundo", was the top goal-scorer in Spain during the 1940s.

2 Johan Cruyff (1947–2016)
Best known for his exploits with Ajax and Barcelona, the Dutch footballer also played for Levante UD *(p58)* in 1981.

3 Mario Kempes (b 1954)
A World Cup winner with Argentina, Kempes appeared in 185 games for Valencia CF, scoring 116 goals.

4 Genovés I (b 1954)
Known as Genovés I after the town in which he was born, Paco Cabanes Pastor has won 14 *pelota* titles.

5 Santiago Canizares (b 1969)
An eccentric but brilliant goalkeeper, Canizares played 445 times for Valencia CF, including the Champions League finals in 2000 and 2001.

6 Álvaro (b 1973)
Known for his punishing left hand, Álvaro Navarro Serra won the Escala i corda singles league six times in a row.

7 Nacho Rodilla (b 1974)
José Ignacio "Nacho" Rodilla Gil spent nine years with Valencia Basket Club and was named MVP in 1998.

8 David Albeda (b 1977)
Valencia-born Albeda spent 15 seasons with Valencia CF, winning two La Liga titles and a European Super Cup.

9 Bojan Dubljević (b 1991)
The Montenegrin was named Most Valuable Player (MVP) when Valencia Basket Club won the league in 2017.

10 Roger Martí (b 1991)
Rising up through the youth ranks at Valencia CF, Martí had a record 49 goals to his name at the end of 2019.

Roger Martí in action

Following pages Pergola filled with bougainvillea in the Jardín de Monforte

🔟 Off The Beaten Track

Bombas Gens Centre d'Art

① Bombas Gens Centre d'Art

Designed by the architect Ramón Esteve, this contemporary art centre *(see p103)* occupies a former factory from the 1930s just north of the Jardín del Turia. Esteve kept the Art Deco façade and used ceramic brick and galvanized steel throughout the gallery as a nod to its industrial past. Works are part of the Fundació Per Amor a l'Art's collection.

② Monasterio de San Miguel de los Reyes

El Escorial, Carlos I's mausoleum near Madrid, was modelled on this impressive complex *(see p105)* in the northern neighbourhood of San Lorenzo. Founded as a Hieronymite monastery by the Duke of Calabria in 1546, it housed political prisoners under Franco and is now the head-quarters of the Valencian Library.

③ Horchatería Daniel

This venerable *horchatería (see p106)* has been going strong since the eponymous Daniel Tortajada first opened its doors in 1979. It is in Alboraya, a small town abutting Valencia to the north, where *chufa*, the tiger nuts used to make the milky drink *horchata* (*orxata* in Valencian) are traditionally grown.

④ Estadi Ciutat de València

MAP E2 ▪ c/de San Vicente de Paúl ▪ www.levanteud.com

Located in the Orriols district, to the northeast of the Centro Histórico, the City of Valencia Stadium is home to Levante Unión Deportiva, Valencia's "other" football team. Despite being the older club, Levante UD compete in the shadow of Valencia CF, although their loyal following means that games can be fun to watch. Tickets to see Las Granotas (the Frogs), as they are known, are not hard to get and can be bought on the gate on the day of the match.

⑤ Trinquet de Pelayo

MAP L5 ▪ c/de Pelayo 6 ▪ www.pelayogastrotrinquet.es

As the home since 1868 of *pelota Valenciana (see p54)*, a handball sport played over a net on a four-sided court *(trinquet)*, this is the best place to catch a game of Escala i corda. Games are usually between teams of two to four players.

The *pelota*-themed restaurant that's part of the Trinquet de Pelayo

Spectators can get incredibly close to the action, sitting on steps on the intimate court and even under the net itself. The Trinquet de Pelayo has its own restaurant.

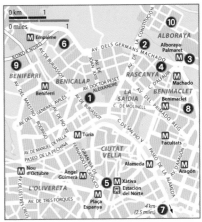

6 Museo del Gremio de Artistas Falleros

Located in the so-called Ciudad Fallera, the Museum of the Guild of Fallas Artists *(see p104)* offers an interesting insight into the spectacular effigies that define Valencia's most famous festival. The museum highlights the creative process, displaying the work of the graphic designers, carpenters, sculptors and painters who produce the *fallas*.

7 Llar Roman
■ Bus 25 from Plaza de la Puerta del Mar, near La Glorieta

Many locals consider this rice restaurant *(see p121)* in the town of Pinedo, just across the diverted Río Turia south of the city, to be the best in Valencia. The owners have been perfecting their tasty Mediterranean dishes – including half a dozen different *paellas* – for more than 40 years.

8 Espai Verd
MAP F3 ■ c/Músico Hipòlito Martínez 16

Uniquely, this Brutalist residential block in the northeast neighbourhood of Benimaclet was designed by the architect Antonio Cortés Ferrando in consultation with the residents who were going to live there. The unusual-looking result is a range of terraced apartments and shops, draped in foliage and with courtyard gardens – Espai Verd means "Green Space". They are stacked higgledy-piggledy on top of one another so that each level receives the maximum amount of sunlight possible.

9 Tavella Restaurant

Dining in Pablo Chirivella's restaurant *(see p107)* in the northern neighbourhood of Beniferri is like having dinner in someone's (beautifully furnished) old home. Behind the large wooden door of this 100-year-old farmhouse, fresh, locally sourced Mediterranean dishes are served at tables laid out around its former living room and kitchen.

10 Lladró

This boutique shop, museum and workshop *(see p106)* in Tavernes Blanques, 15 minutes to the north of the city, showcases the fine porcelain work started by brothers Juan, Vicente and José Lladró in the 1950s. Although they make all kinds of sculptural and decorative art, Lladró are best known for their delicate, and highly detailed, handmade porcelain figurines. The intricacy and level of craftsmanship in the work command high prices.

Vintage Lladró figurine

🔟 Children's Attractions

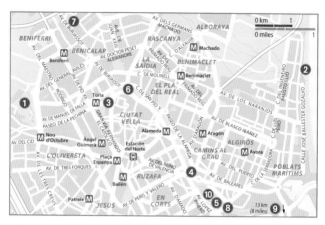

1 BIOPARC

Animals from across Africa graze, swing and stalk around naturalistic enclosures in this conscientous wildlife park (see p104). Different species, interacting much as they would in the wild, are divided across the Savannah, Equatorial Forest, Wetlands and Madagascar areas. There are freqent talks and feedings but be sure to see the lemurs' energetic start to the day.

Meerkat at BIOPARC

2 Beaches

There are three beaches in central Valencia alone, running for 3 km (2 miles) north from the marina in an unbroken ribbon of soft sand (see pp52–3). Facilities include sun-loungers, thatched umbrellas, volleyball nets and pitches for beach football. The promenade that runs behind them is lined with restaurants, tapas bars and shops selling refreshing drinks and ice cream.

3 Teatro la Estrella

This puppet theatre (see p106) is good fun for all ages. The shows, usually fairy tales, take place in the Sala Petxina, a little venue near the Jardín del Turia, which is part museum, part theatre. The puppeteers have been performing for over 30 years, having cut their teeth on TV shows like *Sesame Street*.

4 Parque Gulliver

Children get to play the role of the Lilliputians as they scramble over the prostrate figure of Lemuel Gulliver in this play park (see p23) at the southern end of the Jardín del Turia. In a clever piece of design, Gulliver has been "tied" down with cargo nets and the folds in his clothing serve as steps and slides.

5 Museu de les Ciències

This fully interactive science museum (see p26) is a highlight of the City of Arts and Sciences. Refreshingly, children can be let loose to push, pull, turn and twist almost everything on display here, in particular the practical exhibits that chart the human genome in the Forest of Chromosomes. There is also a fun space simulator (for an additional cost) and a planetarium.

Cycling in the Jardín del Turia

6 Jardín del Turia

This pedestrianized ribbon of green space *(see pp22–3)* is one giant play park for children. It is also a great place to cycle – you can effectively cross Valencia by bike, visiting most of the main sights along the way, without having to worry about traffic. There are also plenty of playgrounds en route, and a fairground sets up close to Alameda metro station in the summer months.

7 Piscina Parque Benicalap

MAP C2 ■ c/Andreu Alfaro 8 ■ Open 8 Jun–8 Sep: noon–6:30pm Mon–Fri, 11am–7pm Sat & Sun ■ Adm

Set in a leafy park in the northern neighbourhood of Benicalap, this low-key water park can become extremely busy at weekends and during the school holidays but is otherwise a fun place to spend an afternoon. There are several pools – including one for toddlers – that feature water slides, splash buckets, a zip wire and an obstacle course. Another pool is for adults only. Sun loungers and umbrellas can be rented, and there is also a picnic area with tables.

8 Oceanogràfic

Giant spider crabs, sea dragons and the bizarre-looking largetooth sawfish are just some of the interesting species on display at this aquarium *(see p26)* in the City of Arts and Sciences. Oceanogràfic houses the largest exhibit of jellyfish in Europe – look out for the aptly named fried-egg jellyfish – as well as a sea turtle rehabilitation centre and several species of shark.

9 Boat Trips on La Albufera

Hire a traditional wooden boat to drift along watery channels and through the reedbeds that fringe this huge freshwater lake in Parque Natural de la Albufera *(see pp36–7)*. There is plenty of birdlife to see out on the water and circling in the thermals overhead, particularly in the morning and late afternoon. Sunset is also a great time to take a trip.

10 Hemisfèric

Roll on water in a large plastic ball on the lake in front of Hemisfèric *(see p27)* in the Ciudad de las Artes e las Ciencias. Afterwards, wow the socks off your kids at a screening at the IMAX. You can watch the film at such an acute angle that it almost feels like lying down. Shows range from space films to natural history documentaries.

Waterballs in front of Hemisfèric

🔟 Bars and Clubs

Wildly ostentatious interior of Barrio del Carmen's Café de las Horas

1 Café de las Horas

Parisian boudoir meets Victorian bordello at this atmospheric bar (see p83) in the historic Barrio del Carmen, extravagantly decorated with chandeliers, velvet curtains, old paintings, statues and overflowing vases. It is a good place to try Agua de Valencia, the local tipple of fresh orange juice, cava, vodka and gin.

2 L'Umbracle Terraza

Part of one of Valencia's most impressive venues, the Umbracle's terrace (see p99) is a spectacular place to while away a balmy Mediterranean evening, with its open-air bar and small dance floor set among plants and palm trees and overlooking the City of Arts and Sciences. There is a downstairs nightclub to move on to.

3 Jimmy Glass Jazz Bar

A serious music venue, Jimmy Glass (see p83) is the longest-running jazz club in Valencia. It is a place that prides itself in securing top musical talent over gimmicky decor – aside from the posters on the walls, this looks like any one of a number of dimly lit bars for which the Barrio del Carmen is famous. There are about four shows a week, featuring both big names and young jazz musicians.

4 Radio City

This long-standing venue (see p83) on Calle Santa Teresa is best known for playing a diverse and eclectic range of musical genres, from flamenco to funk. However, it is much more than that: short films, art exhibitions and theatre also form part of its busy calendar of cultural events.

5 L'Ermità

Enjoying a loyal following, this cosy cultural café *(see p83)* offers a great selection of craft beers. The friendly service helps foster an easy-going atmosphere and there is always something going on, from photography exhibitions and live music to board-games nights and the weekly Drink and Draw workshop.

6 Tyris on Tap

The Centro Histórico outpost for Tyris, a local craft brewer, this bar *(see p83)* offers 10 beers on tap. Each is served with a little side – a glass of Torrija comes with a chunk of chocolate, for example – to be enjoyed either in the industrial-chic interior or on the quiet terrace outside. Tasting racks are available for those who need help deciding.

7 Ubik Café

This café-cum-bookstore *(see p99)* is an archetypal venue for the artsy Ruzafa district. Pull up a chair at one of the mismatched tables and sip a coffee or a craft beer surrounded by second-hand novels and poetry collections. Or drop by for one

Books lining the walls of Ubik Café

of their many events, which include improvised comedy, live music, art exhibitions and children's workshops.

8 Café del Duende

One road back from the Jardín del Turia, this intimate venue *(see p106)* is a fun place to watch some of the best traditional flamenco in Valencia . It's informal but authentic, with two or three dancers holding court on a small stage, spurred on by seated singers and a soulful acoustic guitar player. There are four hour-long shows at the weekend, with a family-friendly early performance every Sunday night.

Café Sant Jaume

9 Café Sant Jaume

It is easy to tell that this legendary café-bar *(see p83)* used to be a pharmacy – the tiny wood-panelled interior, its shelves laden with spirits bottles, still looks like an ancient apothecary. End a wander around the Barrio del Carmen with a quarter-litre jug of Agua de Valencia, made to their own secret recipe, or a sangria on the outside terrace, while watching the comings and goings on bustling Calle Caballeros.

10 Akuarela Playa

This club *(see p112)* on Playa de la Malvarossa comes into its own in summer, when you can dance until dawn beneath the palm trees on the outdoor terrace and watch the sun rise over the Mediterranean before closing time. The four different club spaces play different musical genres, from hip-hop to techno.

▣ Tapas Bars and Restaurants

Lunch at Casa Montaña

1 Casa Montaña

Founded in 1836, this bodega (*see p113*) on a street corner in El Cabanyal is widely regarded as one of the best tapas bars in town. The chefs scour Spain for the finest ingredients – feast on sardines from Cantabria, dry-cured ham from Léon and spicy *patatas bravas* made with potatoes from the Teruel mountains.

2 Ricard Camarena Restaurant

Local celebrity chef Ricard Camarena won a second Michelin star for his eponymous restaurant (*see p107*) in the Bombas Gens Centre d'Art in 2018, only a year after it opened. "Organic" and "local" are the buzzwords in the creative dishes, which place a strong emphasis on vegetables. It seats just 35 people, so booking is essential.

3 Restaurante Navarro

Head to this attractive Mediterranean restaurant (*see p91*) for a relaxing lunch, and try to bag one of the tables out front on the pedestrianized precinct. The menu is a good overview of local Valencian cooking: it is strong on seafood and uses produce bought fresh that morning from the Mercado Central.

4 Restaurante Gordon 10

A laid-back Argentinian steakhouse (*see p101*), this is a carnivore's delight. Choose from generous cuts of meat, sensational steaks and tasty hamburgers, all expertly cooked over a traditional *parrilla* (grill). For a full Argentinian feast, add an *empanada* (filled pastry) and a glass of Malbec.

5 Llar Roman

Customers have to venture outside the city limits to visit this esteemed *arrocería* or rice restaurant (*see p121*), but it is well worth the journey. Paella is their speciality, though this is also a top place to try other classic Valencian rice dishes, such as *arroz de pato*: rice cooked with duck, beans and turnips.

Arroz de pato at Llar Roman

6 Refugio

Taking its name from the location (it stands opposite a former Spanish Civil War air-raid shelter), this imaginative restaurant (*see p85*) in the Barrio del Carmen mixes ingredients from across the world to create fusion dishes such as Iberian pork in a satay sauce or tuna in white miso with jalapeño peppers. The sparse decor contrasts with the bold flavours.

7 La Salvaora

There is an appealing flamenco theme at this charming restaurant *(see p85)* in the heart of the Centro Histórico – black-and-white portraits of historical *figuras* (flamenco stars) grace the walls and soft folk songs play in the background. The food, however, is the real star: a short menu of beautiful Mediterranean dishes that offers excellent value.

8 Nozomi Sushi Bar

A passion for Japanese culture and cuisine shines through at this excellent sushi restaurant *(see p101)*. The cool interior is all bare grey concrete and bamboo lattice screening, designed to resemble a typical (and stylish) Kyoto townhouse. The excellence extends to the menu of delicate tempura, and super-fresh sashimi and sushi.

Sake wines at Nozomi Sushi Bar

9 El Poblet

This polished Michelin-starred restaurant *(see p91)* is headed up by Luís Valls Rozalén, a rising star in Spanish cookery and a disciple of legendary chef Quique Dacosta. Rozalén's imaginative use of typical Valencian ingredients, such as eels, cuttlefish and rice, bear all the creative hallmarks of his mentor.

10 Casa Guillermo

In the fishing quarter of El Cabanyal, this pretty, whitewashed tapas bar *(see p113)* is famous for its anchovies. Try them in a *bocadillo* (sandwich) alongside peppers and olives, or, best of all, served on a plate with olive oil and garlic chunks.

TOP 10 FOOD AND DRINK HIGHLIGHTS

***Esgarrat* on toasted bread**

1 Esgarrat
A delicious combination of cured cod and roasted or grilled red peppers.

2 Clóchinas
These small salty mussels (*clòtxina* in Valencian) are only harvested when there is no "r" in the month.

3 Agua de Valencia
This refreshing local cocktail is made from freshly squeezed orange juice with cava, vodka and gin.

4 All i pebre
A hearty stew from La Albufera of eels and potatoes, cooked in a rich garlic and paprika sauce.

5 Arnadí
This traditional Xàtivan dessert is made with pumpkin and almonds and is shaped like a Moroccan tagine.

6 Fideuà
This seafood dish is similar to classic paella but it is made with thin pasta noodles instead of rice.

7 Horchata
A sweet but refreshing ice-cold drink (*orxata* in Valencian) made from water, sugar and tiger nuts (*chufas*). It is usually accompanied by sweet elongated pastries called *fartons*.

8 Paella
Valencia's most famous dish would traditionally include rabbit, beans and snails; for one layered with fat pink crayfish, order a *paella de marisco*.

9 Suquet de peix
This fish and potato stew originated as a way for fishers to use up the bits they could not sell at the market.

10 Wine
Valencia is home to two Denominación de Origens: Utiel-Requel and Valencia.

TOP 10 Cafés and Cake Shops

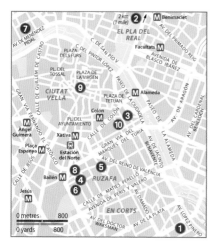

two outlets in the city: aficionados make the trek up to the original café (*see p106*) in Alboroya, once frequented by the Surrealist artist Salvador Dalí, while there is another branch (*see p98*) on the ground floor of the Mercado de Cólon in L'Eixample.

③ La Petite Brioche Sorní

Industrial-chic Brooklyn bistro meets vintage Parisian boulangerie at this cosy bakery (*see p100*) near the Jardín del Turia. Breakfast is a treat here, but it is worth stopping by any time for freshly baked bread, delicious homemade cakes and a range of salads. There's another branch in the Mercado de Abastos.

① La Pequeña Pastelería de Mamá

This welcoming pastry shop (*see p100*) in the Quatre Carreres district, in the south of the city, looks like it has been lifted straight off the pages of a foodie lifestyle magazine. There is a good selection of open sandwiches and *bocadillos* (baguette sandwiches) for brunch or lunch, but it is the picture-perfect fondants and cupcakes that steal the show here.

② Horchatería Daniel

One of the most famous *horchata* producers in Valencia, the artisanal Horchatería Daniel has

④ Café ArtySana

This café (*see p100*) is trendy Ruzafa in a nutshell. A relaxed spot serving wholesome food, it also offers artists a space to showcase their work. Exhibitions, live music, poetry nights and the like provide a buzzy backdrop to the simple, healthy vegetarian and vegan dishes – think beetroot salad; hummus pesto; and

Horchatería Daniel, Mercado de Cólon

Interior of Café ArtySana

goat cheese, honey and walnuts on toast. The good-value three-course brunch and lunch menus include a juice and coffee.

5 Buñoleria Churreria el Contraste

Buñuelos, golden puffs of deep-fried dough, are usually only available during Las Fallas *(see pp34–5)*. However, this unassuming café *(see p100)* in Ruzafa serves them year-round. The delicious snacks are usually made from pumpkin, but come here on a Thursday and it is possible to try their unique orange variety. Their other speciality is crispy, slender *churros*, also deep fried, and dipped in thick chocolate sauce.

6 Dulce de Leche

Named after the caramel confection from Latin America, this Argentinian bakery *(see p100)* has two branches in Valencia, including one in Ruzafa. Visitors will probably not be in the city for too long before they are tempted here by the smorgasbord of tantalizing tarts, strudels, cookies and cakes. It is popular, so be prepared for queues.

7 Dulzumat

There are two branches of this boutique bakery and cake shop *(see p106)* in Valencia, one to the south and the other to the north of the Centro Histórico; both showcase an almost overwhelming number of cakes, pastries and artisanal sweets. A visit here is worth the occasional queue that can form outside.

8 Pastelería Limón y Merengue

Known for its wickedly moreish lemon meringue pies, this French/Italian pastry shop *(see p100)* creates an impressive variety of beautifully crafted cheesecakes, gateaux and fruity tarts. For those looking for something more savoury, they also bake their own sourdough bread, served with homemade preserves.

9 Horchatería de Santa Catalina

This 200-year-old *horchatería (see p84)* is a Valencian institution. The beautiful interior, with its black-and-white checked floor and ceramic tiles from Manises, is a cool retreat from the city heat. Try their signature icy *horchata* or deep-fried, sugar-coated *churros* with chocolate sauce, or drop in on a weekend afternoon for some *buñuelos de calabaza*, a kind of pumpkin fritter.

Horchatería de Santa Catalina

10 Casa Orxata

Specializing in "Bio" *horchata*, made using organic chufa nuts and with no added sugar, this modern *horchatería (see p100)* occupies a prime people-watching spot in the Mercado de Colón. The menu also includes smoothies, milkshakes and crushed-ice drinks, as well as *coca de llanda*, a lemon-drizzle-style cake.

🔟 Places to Shop

The circular Plaza Redonda, lined with traditional craft and souvenir shops

1 Plaza Redonda

Ringed by townhouses, this circular plaza (see p88) is known as El Clot (the Hole) due to its distinctive appearance. Built in 1840 to serve as a fish market, it was restored in 2012 and is now a reliable bet for souvenir shopping, with the ground floor filled with traditional crafts shops.

2 Mercado del Cabanyal

This bustling market (see p109) has served the old fishing quarter since 1958. Seafood, naturally, is the focus and wandering around the fish market while stallholders call out is an essential experience.

3 Poeta Querol
MAP M4

Bisecting the southern Centro Histórico between Calle de la Paz and the Gran Vía, Poeta Querol, once famous for its upmarket boutiques, now offers a wide range of shops to suit all pockets. You'll still find top international brands such as Carolina Herrera and Hugo Boss, along with Spanish labels such as Purificación García, Javier Simorra and the coveted trainer brand, Hoff.

4 Mercado Central

A great place to shop, this marketplace (see pp18–19) houses over 250 stalls with hanging hams, picturesque piles of fruit and vegetable, and a whole variety of seafood fresh from the Mediterranean.

5 Mercado de Tapineria

Much more of a creative collective than a traditional market, this novel gathering of so-called "ephemeral stores" – a cycle of ever-changing pop-up shops – is an interesting place to wander (see p80).

6 Calle de las Cestas
MAP L4

Officially known as Calle Músico Peydró, this narrow side street takes its nickname from the basket weavers who set up their workshops here in

Baskets for sale on Calle de las Cestas

the 1940s and 1950s. "Basket Street" is lined with shops selling straw hats, espadrilles, wicker furniture and, of course, hand-woven baskets.

7 Barrio del Carmen
Shopping in this bohemian district *(see pp12–13)* is an unpredictable pleasure as it is never certain what may turn up in its vintage boutiques, bodegas, art shops and traditional crafts stores.

8 Ruzafa
It is possible to spend hours in this hipster district south of the Centro Histórico, browsing the busy boutiques for vintage clothing, leather-bound books and original artworks. The Mercado de Ruzafa is a typical neighbourhood market with great Valencian products *(see p96)*.

Stalls in Mercado de Ruzafa

9 L'Eixample
MAP N6
The avenues of wealthy L'Eixample are the place for upmarket boutiques. There is expensive shopping to be had on Calle Sorní, Calle Cirilo Amorós and Calle Jorge Juan in the chic neighbourhoods either side of the Gran Vía del Marques del Turia.

10 Shopping Centres
Nuevo Centro: www.nuevo centro.es ■ El Saler: www.elsaler.es ■ Aqua Multiespacio: www.aqua multiespacio.com
Those who would rather shop all under one roof should head to one of Valencia's shopping centres, including Nuevo Centro, El Saler and Aqua Multiespacio.

TOP 10 THINGS TO BUY

Different flavours of turrón

1 Turrón
This chewy almond nougat is a delicious traditional Christmas treat.

2 Vermouth
This herby, fortified wine is ubiquitous in Valencia, where it is drunk on its own as an aperitif or mixed in cocktails.

3 Ceramics
Plates, intricate handmade figurines and decorative blue-and-white tiles (known as *azulejos*) all make for great souvenirs or gifts.

4 Cava
This sparkling wine is produced in Utiel-Requena, a region just to the northwest of Valencia.

5 Charcuterie
The finest grade of jamón serrano (cured ham) is *pata negra*, which is made from free-ranging black pigs fed on a diet of acorns.

6 Jewellery
The exquisite pieces designed by Vicente Gracia on Calle de la Paz have been worn by Queen Sofía of Spain.

7 Paella Pans
Pick up a paella dish from the stalls outside the Mercado Central.

8 Basketry
Wickerwork is one of Valencia's main craft industries. Many wicker products are sold along Calle de las Cestas.

9 Vintage Clothes
The Barrio del Carmen and Ruzafa neighbourhoods are fertile hunting grounds for retro fashion.

10 Wines
Look for red wines from the Denominación de Origen Utiel-Requena that have been produced using the Bobal variety of grape.

🔟 Valencia For Free

The popular Las Arenas beach

1 Beaches
Valencia has three beaches – Playa de las Arenas, Playa de la Patacona and Playa de la Malvarossa *(see pp110–111)* within the city limits and over a dozen more within an hour's drive either side of the city. Most have sun loungers to rent and lifeguards. The city beaches have lots of sports facilities, and from May to October Playa de la Patacona is dotted with *chiringuitos* (beach bars).

2 Free Museums
All of the city-run museums, including La Lonja de la Seda *(see pp20–21)*, Torres de Quart *(see p12)*, Casa-Museo José Benlliure *(see p12)*, Torres de Serranos *(see p13)* and L'ETNO (Museo de Etnologia) *(see p12)* are free on Sundays; the latter is also free on Saturdays. Several other museums offer free entry at certain times of the day: Museo Nacional de Cerámica *(see p88)* after 4pm on Saturday and all day Sunday; and IVAM *(see p13)* from 7 to 9pm on Friday and 3 to 7pm on Saturday.

3 Jardín del Turia
Join a morning yoga class, use the cycle paths as a traffic-free way of moving between the sights or take an early evening stroll beneath the bridges that line the former riverbed of the Río Turia *(see pp22–3)*.

4 Local Festivals
Las Fallas is just the most famous of Valencia's many annual festivals. Whatever the time of year, there will probably be a fiesta going on in one of the city's neighbourhoods, either honouring a saint or celebrating a local tradition, with parades and fireworks *(see pp72–3)*.

5 Museo de Bellas Artes
One of the best fine arts museums in Spain – and certainly with the most diverse collection of Valencian artists in the country – the Museo de Bellas Arts *(see pp30–31)* – is free throughout the year. Temporary exhibitons have included drawings by Antonio Palomino and pottery by Pablo Picasso.

6 Free Concerts at the Palacio des Marqués de Dos Aguas
The first-floor concert ballroom in the lavish Palacio des Marqués de Dos Aguas, the home of the Museo Nacional Cerámica *(see p88)*, provides a memorable setting for free concerts and piano recitals on the last Monday of every month (except August). Seats are first-come, first-served, so be sure to arrive about half an hour early (performances usually start at 8pm).

7 Bird-Watching in La Albufera
The vast marshes, lagoons and forested sand dunes of the Parque Natural de la Albufera *(see pp36–7)* are a

A buzzard in La Albufera

haven for more than 350 species of birds. You can spot them from the hides at the Centro de Interpretación Racó de l'Olla and at the towers that overlook boggy rice fields at Tancat de Mília and Tancat de la Pipa.

8 "Free" Walking Tours

Free Tour Valencia: www. freetourvalencia.com

Free Tour Valencia runs walking tours of the Centro Histórico. They are divided into themes, concentrating on historical monuments, street art or lesser-known sights. You only pay what you think they are worth.

9 Street Art

There is hardly a side alley in the Barrio del Carmen (see pp12–13) that has not had a wall or two covered in murals and oversized paintings. The biggest concentrations of work are around Plaza del Tossal, along Calle Baja and in the Na Jordana area.

Street art in Barrio del Carmen

10 El Tribunal de las Aguas

The Water Court that takes place on Plaza de la Virgen (see p77) dates back more than 1,000 years. Representatives from each of the communities that have formed around the Río Turia's eight main irrigation canals meet outside the cathedral's Puerto de los Apóstoles at noon every Thursday to discuss any disputes (see p78). Always drawing large crowds, the gatherings were designated an Intangible Cultural Heritage by UNESCO in 2009.

TOP 10 BUDGET TIPS

Enjoying lunch at a restaurant

1 During weekday lunchtimes, most restaurants around the city serve a *menú del día* (fixed-price lunch), which offers a good-value option.

2 For an even cheaper lunch option, buy provisions from one of the city's superb markets and enjoy a picnic.

3 In smart restaurants lunchtime meals are usually cheaper than dinner. Several top chefs have informal tapas places as well as their main pricier restaurants.

4 Hotel breakfasts are generally pricey for what you get; bakeries and cafés offer much better value.

5 The Suma 10 ticket (see p124) allows passengers to save around 50 per cent on normal fares. The pass is valid for up to 10 journeys on public transport (bus, metro, local train etc.) and costs €8, depending on how many zones are required.

6 Those who are going to be visiting a lot of museums and using the metro should invest in the excellent Valencia Tourist Card (see p124), which offers free public transport and free entry. Prices start at €15 for a 24-hour card.

7 You can easily see free art outdoors by checking out the awesome murals in the Barrio del Carmen (see p79).

8 Get a bargain meal and battle food waste at the same time with the app Too Good To Go.

9 Several cinemas offer reduced prices on *dia del espectador* (viewer's day), which is usually Wednesday.

10 Many of the city's nightclubs offer free entry to early revellers who arrive before midnight.

TOP 10 Festivals and Events

Plaza de la Virgen during Las Fallas

1 Las Fallas
Various venues ■ **Mar**

Valencia's most famous festival *(see pp34–5)* is a week-long explosion of sound and colour, with marching bands and fireworks providing the backdrop to the *fallas* themselves. These huge monuments are seen as temporary works of art and are often carefully crafted commentaries on the hot topics of the day. The majority go up in flames on the last night of the festival.

2 Semana Santa Marinera
El Cabañyal, Canyamelar, Grao ■ **Easter**

This 10-day celebration of Holy Week is one of the most colourful in Spain. Held on the waterfront, it is focused around the processions of the Brotherhoods of Semana Santa – there are 28 in total. Each represents a different aspect of the Passion of Christ and they sport unusual costumes notable for their coloured robes, hoods and pointy hats.

3 Fiesta de la Virgen de los Desamparados
Centro Histórico ■ **2nd Sun in May**

The image of Our Lady of the Forsaken, one of the patron saints of Valencia, sets off from its home in the basilica on Plaza de la Virgen to be paraded around the Centro Histórico. The icon has its very own vehicle – the number plate (V-0075-GP) is a reference to its nickname, La Geperudeta, or Little Hunchback.

4 Corpus Christi
Various venues ■ **8th Sun after Easter Sun**

This religious festival dates back to 1355 and now includes horseback parades, dances, water fights and a procession of 14th-century carriages shaped like boats.

5 Valencia Pride
Various venues ■ **Jun**

Valencia's annual LGBTQ+ celebration is one of the city's most joyful events. Visitors can expect epic parties, colourful demonstrations and special theatre performances. While the parade is the climax of the event, celebrations take place through the month.

Pride parade in Valencia

6 Noche de San Juan
Valencia beaches ■ **23 & 24 Jun**

Rooted in pagan rituals, the Night of St John is a good excuse for families and friends to gather around bonfires all along Valencia's coast for socializing, singing and dancing. In order to avoid any bad luck over the coming year, participants are meant to jump over waves seven times at midnight before – very carefully – jumping over their bonfire as well.

7 Gran Fería de Valencia
Various venues ■ Jul

The month-long Great Valencia Fair has been celebrated in the city every year since 1871. Concerts, theatre, comedy and spectacular firework displays culminate in the unusual Battle of Flowers, on the last Sunday in July. This is where women dressed in traditional costume are pelted with thousands of carnations, with only tennis rackets for protection.

8 Fiesta del Cristo de la Salud
El Palmar ■ 4 Aug

The highlight of this festival is the afternoon flotilla of boats on La Albufera lake *(see pp36–7)*. The lead vessel carries the image of Cristo de la Salud (Christ of Health) from the town of El Palmar in order to bless the waters and to ensure a bountiful supply of fish for the year ahead.

9 La Tomatina
Buñol ■ Last Wed in Aug

The tiny village of Buñol, 40 km (25 miles) west of Valencia, draws thousands of revellers each year for this epic tomato-throwing festival. Trucks inch their way through the crowded alleyways, dumping hundreds of tonnes of ripe tomatoes onto the streets for a free-for-all.

10 9 October
Various venues ■ 9 Oct

A double celebration, 9 October is both the Day of the Valencian Community, held to commemorate King Jaume I's reconquest of the city, and the Day of St Dionís, Valencia's equivalent of Valentine's Day. The former involves processions from the Town Hall and regional dances.

TOP 10 CELEBRATORY SNACKS

Roscón de Reyes

1 Roscón de Reyes
6 Jan
Round buns topped with candied fruit and containing a small charm.

2 Buñuelos de Calabaza
Mar
Deep-fried pumpkin fritters – the snack of choice during Las Fallas.

3 Torrijas
Holy Week
Slices of bread dipped in beaten egg and cinnamon-laced milk, then fried.

4 Monas de Pascua
Holy Week
"Easter Monkeys" – sweet cakes, baked around a boiled egg.

5 Panquemao
Holy Week
Sweet, fluffy brioche, usually accompanied by a hot chocolate.

6 Sopà d'Aldaia
27 Jul–6 Aug
Dessert prepared during the festivities of Santísimo Cristo de los Necesitados.

7 Pilota de Vallivana
8 Sep
Torpedo-shaped almond confectionery, eaten at the feast of La Madre de Dios de la Vallivana in Picassent.

8 Mocadorà
9 Oct
Small marzipan sweets given to women on the Day of the Valencian Community.

9 Huesos de Santo
1 Nov
White, tubular marzipan sweets eaten on All Saints' Day.

10 Turrón
Christmas
Nougat of different flavours, hard (from Alicante) or soft (from Xixona).

Valencia
Area by Area

The Modernista Mercado de Colón,
a Valencia landmark

🔟 Barrio del Carmen and the Northern Centro Histórico

Many of Valencia's major sights, spanning the city's history from its founding in 138 BCE, are located in the northern half of the Centro Histórico, or Old Town (Ciutat Vella in Valencian). Much of the original Roman forum can be seen in La Almoina; there are traces of the old wall that used to divide the Islamic and Christian quarters here; and the city's remaining medieval gateways bookend the absorbing Barrio del Carmen. This half of the Centro Histórico is also home to the Gothic-style cathedral and the seat of regional government.

Iglesia de San Juan del Hospital

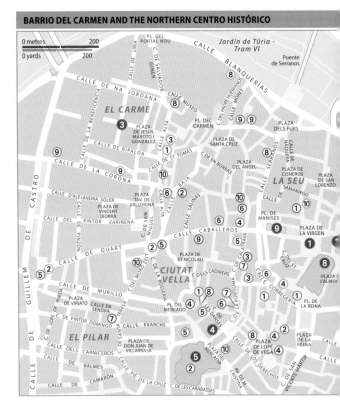

BARRIO DEL CARMEN AND THE NORTHERN CENTRO HISTÓRICO

Fountain in Plaza de la Virgen

1 Plaza de la Virgen
MAP M2

This lovely square is always busy with people visiting the cathedral, paying their respects to Our Lady of the Forsaken in the Basílica de la Virgen de los Desamparados. It has a fine central fountain, and there are plenty of cafés and bars around its fringes. The plaza is a focal point of the Las Fallas festival, when a huge wooden statue of the Virgin Mary is adorned in flowers (see p34).

2 La Almoina
MAP M2 ■ Plaza Décimo Junio Bruto ■ Open 10am–7pm Mon–Sat, 10am–2pm Sun ■ Adm; free Sun

Set on a Roman square and charting 2,000 years of Valencia's history, this museum is the fruit of 20 years of archaeological excavations. Elevated walkways lead through the remains of a central forum, basilica and Roman baths, given added atmosphere by the water-covered glass roof above them. There are also buildings from Valencia's time under the Visigoths, such as the nearby chapel outside the museum, and from its Islamic era. The Almoina building itself was a medieval Christian institution for distributing food among the poor.

3 Barrio del Carmen
Brimming with character, this fascinating neighbourhood (see pp12–13) is home to great museums, contemporary art centres, churches and the remnants of the old city walls.

4 La Lonja de la Seda
It took the finest crafters over 60 years to complete the 16th-century Silk Exchange (see pp20–21). A reminder of Valencia's most flourishing artistic period, it is the city's only UNESCO World Heritage Site.

Inner courtyard of La Lonja

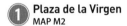

Stalls under the central dome inside the Mercado Central

5 Mercado Central

This vast Modernista market *(see pp18–19)* is an unforgettable place to browse. Its sun-filled interior of vaulted iron beams, patterned tiles and stained-glass windows is home to a whole host of stalls of the finest and freshest local produce.

6 Baños del Almirante

MAP M3 ■ c/Baños del Almirante 3 ■ Closed for restoration

The last remaining Arab baths in Valencia, the Baños del Almirante were built at the beginning of the 14th century following the traditional design of an Islamic hammam. They were in use right up to 1959, and then as a gym until the city council bought the building in 1985 and refurbished it. There is inadequate signage, but it is quite atmospheric, with its arched Mudéjar doorway and star-ceilinged main dome.

7 Iglesia de San Juan del Hospital

MAP M3 ■ c/Trinquete de Caballeros 5 ■ Open 6:45–7:45am, 9:30am–1:30pm & 5–9pm Mon–Fri; 9:30am– 1:30pm & 5–9pm Sat; 11am–2pm & 5–9pm Sun

Unusually well-preserved for its age, this hospital church dates back to the Reconquest, when King Jaume I ordered its construction to thank the religious-military Order of St John of Jerusalem for their help during his successful campaign against Muslim rule. The church contains beautiful Romanesque, Mudéjar, Gothic and Baroque features, the latter most notably in the ornamental chapel of Santa Barbara.

8 La Catedral

Valencia's dominant central cathedral *(see pp14–17)* runs through a whole spectrum of architectural eras, taking in Romanesque doorways, a vast, dark Gothic interior and a florid Baroque façade. The jewelled chalice in one of its many interesting side chapels may or may not be the Holy Grail, but there is no disputing the magnificent views that can be

---

EL TRIBUNAL DE LAS AGUAS

Thought to be the oldest judicial institution in Europe, the Tribunal de las Aguas deals with issues relating to the *acequias* (irrigation ditches) that divert water from the Río Turia. It takes place every Thursday at noon outside La Catedral's Puerto de los Apóstoles. The colourful proceedings are always in Valencian and only ever oral, and all disputes are settled then and there.

had from the adjoining El Miguelete bell tower, reaching across the rooftops of the Centro Histórico.

⑨ Palau de la Generalitat

MAP L2 ■ c/Caballeros 2
■ 963 424 636 ■ Guided tours
Mon–Fri; book in advance

This towered Gothic palace is the official seat of the Valencia Regional Government. It was built in 1482 by Pere Compte, the master architect responsible for La Lonja de la Seda, and is named after the taxes created by King Pedro III of Aragon, known as *generalitats* – the palace became the headquarters of the institution founded to collect them. The guided tours visit a few key rooms, including the Golden Hall, with its magnificent golden coffered ceiling, and the Parliament Hall, whose walls are covered with paintings representing the different historical branches (ecclesiastical, military and civil) of the Valencian government.

Golden Hall, Palau de la Generalitat

⑩ Centro Cultural Bancaja

MAP N3 ■ Plaza de Tetuan 23
■ Open 9am–2pm & 4–9pm Mon–Fri, 10am–2pm & 4–8pm Sat & Sun
■ Adm; under 12s free

This cultural centre provides a multidisciplinary space for temporary exhibitions and for conferences and workshops organized by the Fundación Bancaja, the Spanish bank's non-profit arm. There are often big names on show; past exhibitions have included work by Pablo Picasso and Joaquín Sorolla.

A MORNING STREET ART TOUR OF BARRIO DEL CARMEN

▶ Start at Plaza del Tossal, with its two striking wall murals: *Moses*, by the Italian artist Blu, has a nest of snakes for a beard; the cars tumbling down the adjacent building are the minimalist work of Escif, the "Spanish Banksy". Across the square, Fasim's *Stop War – Victim's Wall* has shades of Pablo Picasso's *Guernica*.

Head down the street opposite Café Sant Jaume until it forks. Chilean artist Disneylexia reinterprets ancient mythology in his murals, as seen in the Egyptian/Aztec mash-up on the corner of Calle Alta and Calle Baja. Walk along Calle Baja – keeping an eye out for David de Limón's ninjas, who are clad in balaclavas and wield aerosol cans – and stay right when you get to the small square with an olive tree in its centre. You are now on Calle del Pintor Fillol, where Julieta XLF's distinctive *kawaii* (the Japanese culture of cuteness) character adorns the Bed & Bike shop on the right-hand side.

Turn right at Plaza del Carmen, then first left onto Calle Moret, known as Calle de los Colores after its profusion of murals. Backtrack to Plaza del Carmen, then turn left onto Calle Alta and follow it back towards Plaza del Tossal. Turning right by the fire station ("*Bombers*") you'll reach Plaza Tavernes de Valldigna, home to Deih's mummified zombie and a horse being pulled by giant snails. Then follow Calle de San Miguel to Plaza Tossal, stopping for a well-earned drink at **Café Sant Jaume** *(see p83)* to round off your tour of Barrio del Carmen's street art.

See map on pp76–7

The Best of the Rest

The colourful Mercado de Tapineria

1 Mercado de Tapineria
MAP L3 ■ c/Tapineria 15–17
■ www.mercadodetapineria.com
From exhibitions to temporary shops, there's always something different happening in this market.

2 Galeria del Tossal
MAP K2 ■ Plaza del Tossal
■ Open 4–7pm Tue–Sat, 10am–2pm Sun ■ Adm; free Sat & Sun
The art here is displayed around the remains of the 12th-century Islamic city walls.

3 Almudín
MAP M2 ■ Plaza San Luis Beltrán ■ Open 10am–2pm & 3–7pm Tue–Sat, 10am–2pm Sun ■ Adm; free Sat & Sun
This 14th-century granary houses temporary art exhibitions.

4 Iglesia de Santa Catalina
MAP L3 ■ Plaza de Santa Catalina ■ Open 10am–1pm & 7–8pm daily
According to legend, the belfry of this church is "married" to La Catedral's El Miguelete tower.

5 Iglesia de los Santos Juanes
MAP L3 ■ Plaza del Mercado
Next to Mercado Central, this Baroque church has a distinctive triangular-shaped clock tower.

6 L'Iber
MAP L2
■ c/Caballeros 20–22
■ Open 11am–2pm & 4–7pm Wed–Sun (to 2pm Sun in winter)
■ Adm ■ www.museo liber.org
The unique Museum of Lead Soldiers features nearly 100,000 toy figures, laid out to depict major battles and campaigns in history.

7 Espacio Inestable
MAP M2 ■ c/Aparisi y Guijarro 7
■ www.espacioinestable.com
The "Volatile Space" theatre company produces mostly avant-garde theatre and dance performances.

8 Refugio Antiaereo de Serranos
MAP L2 ■ c/Serranos ■ 962 081 390 ■ Tours 10am, noon, 4pm & 5pm Tue, 10am & noon Sat (phone ahead)
This well-preserved air-raid shelter provided safe refuge for up to 400 people at a time during the Spanish Civil War.

9 Museo de Prehistoria de Valencia
MAP K2 ■ Centro Cultural La Beneficència, c/de la Corona
■ Open 10am–8pm Tue–Sun
■ Adm ■ www.mupreva.org
This archeological museum covers Paleolithic times, Iberian culture and Roman Valencia.

10 Mercado Mossén Sorrell
MAP K2 ■ Plaza Mossén Sorrell
■ Open 8am–3pm Mon–Wed & Sat, 8am–3pm & 5–8pm Thu–Fri
Dating back to the 1920s, this market has become a famous spot for gourmet delights and offers a host of activities from wine-tastings to cooking demonstrations.

See map on pp76–7

Mercado Central Stalls

① Jose Berenguer
Stalls 133 & 134 ▪ Open 7:30am–3pm Mon–Sat

This stall is packed with hanging hams and dry-cured meats. Try a few slices of *jamón ibérico de bellota*.

② Delicias Verdes
Stalls 254–258 ▪ Open 7:30am–3pm Mon–Sat

A good place to shop for vegetables from La Huerta: huge peppers, fat Valencian tomatoes, plus *bajoquetes* and *garrofones*, the beans used in traditional paella dishes.

③ Solaz
Stalls 57–64 ▪ Open 7:30am–3pm Mon–Sat

The go-to stall for the city's chefs, who shop here for cheeses such as Espadán de Los Corrales, a goat cheese from the Sierra de Espadán.

④ Caracoles Peribañez
Stalls 287–289 ▪ Open 7:30am–3pm Mon–Sat

It is quite hard to miss this stall, the only one in the market that sells *caracoles* (snails). There are several varieties on offer, all stacked in crates and attempting in vain to slither out of their netted bags.

⑤ Pescados Pepa Puerto
Stalls 1–5 ▪ Open 7:30am–3pm Mon–Sat

This is where you'll find delicacies such as the much-prized red prawns from Dénia, as well as tempting displays of the latest catch.

⑥ Mercat Divi
Stalls 117–119 ▪ Open 7:30am–3pm Mon–Sat

This little boutique specializes in Valencian wines but also does artisanal oils, vinegars and salts.

⑦ La Parada de las Especias
Stalls 414–416 ▪ Open 7:30am–3pm Mon–Sat ▪ www.comprarespecias.net

Older than the market itself, this stall has been going strong for 125 years and sells saffron, smoked paprika and all sorts of spices.

⑧ Frutas Virginia
Stalls 83–88 ▪ Open 7:30am–3pm Mon–Sat

Among the many fruit stalls, this is the largest and most colourful, stacked with seasonal fruits.

⑨ La Casquería de Angela
Stalls 15 & 16 ▪ Open 7:30am–3pm Mon–Sat

Not for the weak-stomached, this offal stall sells pigs' trotters, brain, tripe and sheep's heads.

⑩ Las Paellas del Mercado Central
Stalls 6, 8 & 10 ▪ Open 7:30am–3pm Mon–Sat

Located just outside the market itself, this is the place to come to buy a paella pan, from four-person dishes through to gigantic pans that would feed a small village.

Local seafood in the Fish Market

Shops

1 Simple
MAP M2 ■ c/de Palacio 5
■ www.simple.com.es
An Aladdin's Cave of artisanal products, all crafted in Spain. Forage for locally woven shopping bags, Manises ceramics and wool scarves made in the White Towns of Andalucia.

2 Artesanía Yuste
MAP L3 ■ Plaza del Milagro del Mocadoret
Hand-painted ceramic figures, tiles and bowls are on sale here, many of them made by the friendly owner and his son.

3 Bodegas Baviera
MAP L3 ■ c/de Corregería 40
Established in 1870, the family-run Bodegas Baviera can lay claim to being Valencia's oldest wine shop.

4 Atypical Valencia
MAP L2 ■ c/de Caballeros 10
■ www.atypicalvalencia.com
As the name suggests, the knick-knacks in this gift shop are far from everyday souvenirs. There are retro prints of Valencia's iconic buildings, mosaic maps and distincitve tote bags.

5 La Postalera
MAP L3 ■ c/Danzas 3
■ www.lapostalera.es
This colourful boutique showcases an original range of badges, bags, magnets, postcards and cushions.

6 Santo Spirito Vintage
MAP L2 ■ c/de Alta 22
■ www.santospiritovintage.com
A one-stop shop for bargain retro Americana, this vintage store stocks Hawaiian shirts, denim jackets and its own range of hip streetwear.

7 AlVent
MAP L2 ■ c/Calatrava 4
■ www.alvent.com
Bedecked in flowers, this charming jewellery shop is a lovely place to browse for delicate one-off pieces, from moonstone rings to bubble anklets.

8 Kúbelik
MAP M3 ■ c/dels Drets, 36
■ www.kubelik.es
This tiny clothing store has original and striking designs, with an emphasis on sustainable fabrics .The clothes are made in Valencia with natural fabric and promote ethical production. It also has a small collection of quirky jewellery and accessories.

9 Cecilia Plaza Handmade
MAP L1 ■ c/Roteros 14
■ www.ceciliaplaza.com
Original and quirky, this gift shop is full of bags, cushions, posters, prints and toys, all designed with charm by the artist owner.

La Postalera gift shop

10 Original CV
MAP L3 ■ Plaza del Mercado 35 ■ www.originalcv.es
Pop into this former pharmacy, dating from 1880, to stock up on traditional Valencian products such as Bobal wine from Utiel-Requena, Bomba rice from La Albufera, tiger nuts, cheese, honey and turrón.

Bars and Clubs

(1) Café de las Horas
MAP M2 ■ c/Conde de Almodóvar 1 ■ www.cafede lashoras.com

The over-the-top Baroque decor at this bar just north of Plaza de la Virgen makes for an atmospheric setting in which to enjoy a gin and tonic or two, or cocktails and a cake.

(2) Jimmy Glass Jazz Bar
MAP L2 ■ c/Baja 28
■ www.jimmyglassjazz.net

A favourite fixture on Valencia's jazz circuit, this intimate place hosts performances by local artists, touring trios and international acts, mostly playing modern jazz.

(3) Café Negrito
MAP L2 ■ Plaza Negrito

A cocktail in this modern bar is a great way to start off the evening, especially if you can get one of the tables on its lovely little plaza.

(4) Tyris on Tap
MAP L3 ■ c/Taula de Canvis 6
■ www.cervezatyris.com

This laid-back microbrewery does a good range of craft beers, including their own lagers, brown ales and IPAs.

(5) Café Sant Jaume
MAP K2 ■ c/de Caballeros 51

One of the Barrio del Carmen's first cafés when it opened over 30 years ago, the iconic Café Sant Jaume is a great place to grab a coffee or something a little stronger – they are known for their Agua de Valencia cocktail – either in the tiny bar itself or at the tables on the plaza outside.

(6) L'Ermità
MAP K2 ■ c/Obispo Don Jerónimo 4

With a welcoming, snug interior and a pleasant little terrace, L'Ermità is often full of regulars drawn here by the programme of live music and other events and performances.

(7) Radio City
MAP K2 ■ c/de Santa Teresa 19
■ www.radiocityvalencia.es

Whether it is reggae, funk, theatre, flamenco or jazz, there is always something going on here. The music and great cocktails help attract a diverse and easy-going clientele.

Live music performance at Radio City

(8) The Market Craft Beer
MAP L3 ■ c/Cajeros 1

The friendly staff here will help customers pick out an ideal pint from their wide range of international IPAs and other craft ales, which include several Valencian and Spanish brews.

(9) Fox Congo
MAP L3 ■ c/de Caballeros 35

Consistently good music and efficient and friendly service behind the bar make this nightclub one of the most popular places for a late-night dance in the Barrio del Carmen.

(10) GONG
MAP L3 ■ c/de la Concordia 3

The music in this retro underground bar is almost as eclectic as the decor and covers many styles and eras from soul and blues to funk and boogaloo.

See map on pp76–7 ←

Tapas Bars and Cafés

Colmado LaLola tapas restaurant

1 Colmado LaLola
MAP L2 ■ c/Bordadores 10
■ www.lalolarestaurante.com ■ €

This delicatessen and restaurant harks back to Valencia's *botigas* (little stores) of old, where the tapas are chalked up on blackboards and the jamón serrano is sliced in front of you.

2 Central Bar
MAP L3 ■ Mercado Central
■ Closed Sun ■ www.centralbar.es ■ €

The freshest produce is guaranteed at this tapas bar in the heart of the Mercado Central, where chef Ricard Camarena's food is available for a fraction of his restaurants' prices.

3 Taberna La Samorra
MAP M2 ■ c/Almudín 14

This classic tapas bar offers a range of local specialities and more substantial dishes. The wine list includes plenty of options from the Valencia region.

4 Horchatería Santa de Catalina
MAP L3 ■ Plaza de Santa Catalina 6 ■ www.horchateria santacatalina.com ■ €

One of the oldest *horchaterías* in Valencia, this is a lovely spot to grab a *horchata*, regular or *granizado* (with crushed ice), some *churros* or a scoop of artisanal ice cream.

5 Mayan Coffees
MAP K2 ■ c/Murrillo 54
■ 722 788 433 ■ €

This coffeeshop roasts gourmet beans from the owner's estate in Guatemala, plus varieties from Mexico, Peru, Costa Rica and Colombia. Great fruit juices, too.

6 Taberna La Sénia
MAP L3 ■ c/de la Cenia 2
■ www.tabernalasenia.es ■ €

Named after the watermill that used to exist here, this cosy tavern serves fresh, varied tapas, with ingredients sourced from the Mercado Central.

7 Tasca Angel
MAP L3 ■ c/Purisima 1
■ 963 917 835 ■ Closed Sun ■ €

A simple *tasca* (cheap bar), this spot has carved out a reputation for serving the best sardines in Valencia.

8 Café Museu
MAP L1 ■ c/Museo 7 ■ 960 725 047 ■ Closed Mon ■ €

Just off Plaza del Carmen, this café is the perfect spot for a quick bite (try the tortillas).

9 Almalibre Açaí House
MAP L1 ■ c/Roteros 16
■ Closed Mon ■ www. almalibreacaihouse.com/ valencia ■ €

Açaí bowls can be created to taste at this vegetarian place. There are other savoury options piled high with healthy combinations.

Breakfast bowl at Almalibre Açaí Bar

10 La Pilareta
MAP K2
■ c/de Moro Zeid 13 ■ www. barlapilareta.es ■ €

This bustling, no-frills tapas joint, also known as Bar Pilar, is famous for its *clochinas* – small, sweet local mussels. The shells are discarded into buckets placed strategically along the bottom of the bar.

Restaurants

PRICE CATEGORIES

For a three-course meal for one with half a bottle of wine (or equivalent meal), taxes and extra charges.

€ under €35 €€ €35–60 €€€ over €60

1 Refugio
MAP K2 ▪ c/Alta 42 ▪ www.refugiorestaurante.com ▪ €€

The simple decor belies the unusual food combinations here, where mains like duck magret mix Asian spices with Latin American sauces.

2 Restaurante Canela
MAP J2 ▪ c/de Quart 49 ▪ www.restaurantecanela.es ▪ Closed Mon ▪ €

A good option for traditional local cuisine, this smart restaurant specializes in rice dishes and seafood.

3 La Marrana
MAP K2 ▪ c/Alta ▪ Closed Mon & Tue ▪ www.lamarrana.com ▪ €

The highlights at this friendly tavern include delicious platters of local cheese, chilled *salmorejo* soup and *ropa vieja* (a slow-cooked Cuban stew). There's a secret terrace where visitors enjoy a peaceful respite.

4 La Pappardella
MAP L2 ▪ c/Bordadores 6 ▪ www.restaurantelapappardella.com ▪ €

A very central location (it is in the shadow of the cathedral belfry) at which to enjoy fresh pastas dishes.

5 La Salvaora
MAP M2 ▪ c/Calatrava 19 ▪ www.lasalvaora.com ▪ €€

This atmospheric Mediterranean restaurant is always busy thanks to the quality of its cooking. The tasting menu is excellent value.

6 Tinta Fino Ultramarino
MAP L3 ▪ c/Corretgeria 38

A cosy, colourful restaurant, this spot serves a mix of Italian and Mediterranean tapas, prepared with a creative touch. There are several vegetarian options and a wide selection of wines.

7 Secreter
MAP M2 ▪ c/los Maestres 5 ▪ Closed D Mon–Thu; all day Sun ▪ www.secretersaladeestar.com ▪ €

A relaxed, informal restaurant, Secreter serves locally sourced food.

8 Restaurant Blanqueries
MAP L1 ▪ c/Blanquerías 12 ▪ Closed Mon ▪ www.restauranteblanqueries.com ▪ €€

The chefs here, trained at El Bulli and Arzak, create memorable Spanish dishes made with local produce.

9 Thai Mongkut
MAP K2 ▪ c/de la Corona 8 ▪ Closed Mon ▪ www.thaimongkut.es

Fragrant Thai dishes are served in this gorgeous restaurant that would not look out of place in Bangkok.

10 Kuzina
MAP M2 ▪ c/Conde de Almodóvar 4 ▪ Closed Tue ▪ www.kuzinavlc.com ▪ €€

This traditional Greek restaurant offers a good choice of meze.

Tables outside Kuzina

See map on pp76–7

🔟 The Southern Centro Histórico

The southern half of the Old Town developed after the Reconquest in the 13th century, as the Christian city spread beyond what was then known as Balansiya. For the most part, the streets here are wider and less tangled than those in the Barrio del Carmen and the old Islamic quarter. Today, the area is the commercial hub of Valencia, with the streets around Calle Poeta Querol, Calle Juan de Austria and Calle Colón forming the city's premier shopping district. The focal point is the Plaza del Ayuntamiento, Valencia's grand main square and the location of the Town Hall and Neo-Classical Post Office. The square is well served by buses, and there is easy access to the metro, with stations at Colón, Xàtiva and Àngel Guimerà.

Statue of Juan Luis Vives, by Josep Aixa Íñigo, Centro Cultural La Nau

THE SOUTHERN CENTRO HISTÓRICO

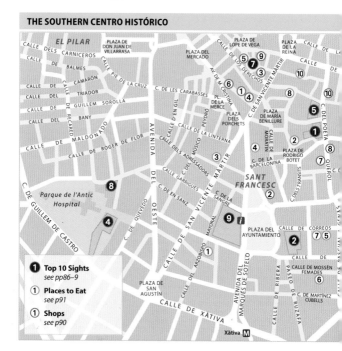

1 Top 10 Sights
see pp86–9

1 Places to Eat
see p91

1 Shops
see p90

1 Iglesia de San Juan de la Cruz

MAP M3 ▪ c/Poeta Querol 6

Dedicated to St John of the Cross, this church was built on the site of a mosque and was one of the first to be consecrated after the Reconquest of Valencia. It was reopened only in 2010 after being closed for extensive renovations for more than half a century, works that restored the Rococo interior to its full glory. Note that the entrance is actually on Calle San Andrés.

2 Edificio de Correos y Telégrafos

MAP M4 ▪ Plaza del Ayuntamiento 24 ▪ Closed Sun

Easily recognized by its cast-iron telegraph tower, Valencia's Neo-Classical Post Office was built in the first half of the 20th century. The elegant façade bears sculptures that are rich in allegory: five figures, representing Europe, Asia, Africa,

The Edificio de Correos y Telégrafos

America and Oceania; and angels carrying messages by land (train) and sea (ship). The impressive interior is capped by a stained-glass dome featuring the shields of the 48 Spanish provinces.

3 Centro Cultural La Nau

MAP M3 ▪ c/de la Nave ▪ Exhibition Hall closed Mon ▪ www.uv.es/cultura

This 15th-century edifice, built by the master architect Pere Compte, serves as the cultural centre for the University of Valencia. Visitors can wander around the Neo-Classical cloisters and view the latest exhibitions in the Sala Estudi General – previous shows have included the works of Valencian painter Artur Heras and Argentinian photographer Humberto Rivas. Their programme of performing arts includes music and film festivals.

4 Museo Valenciano de la Ilustración y la Modernidad (MuVIM)

MAP K4 ▪ c/Quevedo 10 y Guillem de Castro 8 ▪ Closed Mon ▪ www. muvim.es

The Valencian Museum of the Enlightenment and Modernity is essentially a museum of ideas. The main permanent exhibition is the hour-long Adventure of Thought, a theatrical mix of costumed actors and audiovisual exhibits that seek to explore some key developments in thinking over the last 500 years, from the Theocentrism of the Middle Ages to the modern science of today.

⑤ Museo Nacional de Cerámica

MAP M3 ▪ c/Poeta Querol 2 ▪ 963 08 54 29 ▪ Open 10am–2pm & 4–8pm Tue–Sat, 10am–2pm Sun ▪ Adm; free Sat pm & Sun

Occupying the Palacio del Marqués de Dos Aguas (see p46), considered the best example of Baroque architecture in Spain, this museum houses an enormous collection of ceramics. Covering everything from prehistoric and early Islamic earthenware to Valencian pottery's 15th-century heyday and modern designs, the ceramic displays take up the third floor. Take time to also explore the palace's sumptuous rooms, including the ballroom and boudoir, and see the marquis's collection of ornate ceremonial carriages.

⑥ Real Colegio Seminario de Corpus Christi

MAP M3 ▪ c/la Nave 1 ▪ 963 514 176 ▪ Open 11am–1:30pm & 5–7pm Mon–Fri, 11am–1:30pm Sat & Sun ▪ Adm ▪ www.seminariocorpuschristi.org

Founded in the 16th century by Juan de Ribera, the influential reformist Archbishop of Valencia, this seminary is still home to monks, who perform Gregorian Mass in the beautiful, fresco-covered church each afternoon. Outside these hours, you can visit the church, as well as the Renaissance cloisters and the Museo del Patriarca, home to Ribera's collection of works by Van der Weyden, Caravaggio and

Pinazo. Best of all, though, is the Chapel of the Monument, whose ceiling and walls are decorated with scenes from the *Sacrifice of the Cross* by Tomás Hernández and some fine 16th-century Flemish tapestries. Try not to miss the "Dragon of the Patriarch" on the way in, actually a crocodile brought back by Spanish missionaries from Latin America.

⑦ Plaza Redonda

MAP L3

Situated in a web of alleyways south of the cathedral and encircled by craft shops and tapas bars, the circular Plaza Redonda looks more like a bull ring than a city square. The plaza's historical names have been engraved around the central fountain, along with a quote from Valencia-born writer Vicente Blasco Ibáñez.

⑧ Museo y Colegio del Arte Mayor de la Seda

MAP K4 ▪ c/Hospital 7 ▪ Open 10am–7pm Tue–Sat, 10am–2:30pm Sun ▪ Adm ▪ www.museodelaseda valencia.com

In the mid-18th century, half the city's population was employed in the silk trade. This museum occupies a restored Gothic building that has served as the headquarters of the College of High Silk Art since the 15th century. The exhibits cover the silk production process and chart the development of elaborate costumes through the ages (see p48). Temporary exhibitions are held in the

Museo del Patriarca, Real Colegio Seminario de Corpus Christi

upstairs Salón de la Fama, notable for its ceramic floor and ceiling fresco, both created in 1757.

9 Ayuntamiento
MAP L4 ■ Plaza del Ayuntamiento 1 ■ Closed for restoration

Francisco Mora Berenguer's Neo-Classical Town Hall was built between 1905 and 1929. Highlights include the Baroque Salón de Fiestas, with its vast bohemian chandeliers, and the Museo Histórico Municipal, whose collection includes old city maps, the flag used during the Reconquest and the Conqueror King's sword.

Salón de Fiestas, Ayuntamiento

10 Luis Adelantado
MAP N3 ■ c/Bonaire 6 ■ Open 10am–2pm & 4–8pm Mon–Fri, Sat by appointment ■ www.luisadelantadovlc.com

The stark, whitewashed walls and dark marble floors of this striking contemporary art gallery provide the perfect canvas for exhibitions from national and international artists. All of the building's five floors are used for displaying temporary shows, which allows for plenty of variety and some grand set-piece installations.

ESTRECHA

Head through the gateway on the northwest of Plaza Redonda and look for a terracotta-coloured strip wedged into the opposite side of Plaza Lope de Vega. Measuring just 107 cm (42 inches) wide, this is reputedly one of the narrowest houses in Europe. See old photos of it in the adjacent tapas bar.

A MORNING'S WANDER AROUND THE SHOPPING DISTRICT

From the bottom of Plaza de la Reina, head along Calle Paz and turn right onto Calle del Marqués de Dos Aguas, home to fashion emporiums such as Boss Store, on the corner, and **Loewe**, at No 7 *(see p90)*. The street soon morphs into Calle Poeta Querol, an upmarket stretch with top international brands and more accessible labels from Spain. Admire the elegant dresses at local designer, **Isabel Sanchis** (No 5), before taking a coffee break at **Federal Valencia** nearby *(see p91)*.

Return to Poeta Querol to marvel at the graceful porcelain sculptures in **Lladró Boutique** (No 9) *(see p90)* and the exquisite jewellery at **Barack** (No 2) *(see p90)* before checking out the brilliant designs favoured by Spanish celebrities at Koker (No 12). Turn left onto Calle Juan de Austria, where the more budget-friendly Spanish high-street favourites, Tezenis (No 28) and Mango (No 7) can be found, along with an array of different shoe shops – try Zapa (No 34) or Ulanka (No 9).

For those who are feeling flush, cross Calle Colón and head down Calle Jorge Juan, which has taken over from c/ Poeta Querol as Valencia's new "Golden Mile", to shop at top Spanish designers such as Purificación García (No 10) and Bimba y Lola (No 17). Otherwise, for more affordable options walk along Calle Colón, the road that marks the Centro Histórico's southern border, and take a pick from dozens of high-street fashion brands, from Camper (No 13) to Lacoste (No 52).

See map on pp86–7

Shops

1 Librería Anticuaria Rafael Solaz

MAP L3 ▪ c/San Fernando 7 ▪ www.libreriarafaelsolaz.es

It is easy to spend hours browsing through this wonderful traditional bookstore, with shelves of discontinued, rare or just unusual and antique curiosities.

2 ALE-HOP

MAP L4 ▪ Plaza del Ayuntamiento 19 ▪ www.ale-hop.net

This Spanish chain is famous for the black-and-white cows that guard the entrances to its shops. Their Plaza del Ayuntamiento branch is one of several in Valencia, each full of quirky gifts and knick-knacks.

3 Las Ollas de Hierro

MAP L3 ▪ c/Derechos 4 ▪ www.tiendadelasollasdehierro.com

The oldest shop in Valencia, Las Ollas was founded in 1793 and still retains its original wooden interior. The store sells haberdashery, jewellery, religious items and souvenirs.

4 La Petite Planèthé

MAP L3 ▪ c/San Fernando 4 ▪ www.lapetiteplanethe.com

More than 200 varieties of tea, infusions and artisan coffees can be found at this fine tea shop.

La Petite Planèthé

5 Colla Monlleó

MAP L3 ▪ Plaza Redonda 12–13

Split into two little boutiques, one on either side of an archway leading to the Plaza Redonda, this family-run ceramics shop sells items from fridge magnets and wall hangings to hand-crafted plates and religious statues.

A decorative plate from Colla Monlleó

6 Sebastian Melmoth

MAP L3 ▪ c/San Fernando 17

This art-and-design store sells a great variety of unusual collectibles and also doubles as a gallery and exhibition space for local artists.

7 Barack

MAP M4 ▪ c/Salvá 2 ▪ www.barackbyzelma.com

Barack's high-end jewellery often features big semiprecious stones. The Duchess of Sussex and Selma Hayek are clients.

8 Lladró Boutique

MAP M4 ▪ c/Poeta Querol 9 ▪ www.lladro.com

For those who cannot get out to the main shop and museum in Tavernes Blanques (see p106), this outlet is the place to see the porcelain sculptures that have made Lladró a global name.

9 La Casa de Los Botijos

MAP L3 ▪ Plaza Redonda 14 ▪ Closed Sun

The fourth-generation owners of this ceramics shop sell Sargadelo crockery, baked socarrat tiles and botijos (decorative earthenware jars).

10 Loewe

MAP M3 ▪ c/del Marqués de Dos Aguas 7 ▪ www.loewe.com

A range of stylish accessories and bags is available from this long-running Spanish fashion house, which opened its first shop in 1846.

Places to Eat

PRICE CATEGORIES

For a three-course meal for one with half a bottle of wine (or equivalent meal), taxes and extra charges.

€ under €35   €€ €35–60   €€€ over €60

1 Restaurante Navarro
MAP L4 ■ c/Arzobispo Mayoral 5 ■ Closed D; all day Sun ■ www.restaurantenavarro.com ■ €€

Handed down through the family since 1951, this Mediterranean restaurant is recommended for its classic Valencian rice dishes.

2 Federal Valencia
MAP M4 ■ c/Embajador Vich 15 ■ 960 617 956 ■ €

The Valencian branch of this coffee shop is famous for its strong roasts, but it is also an appealing place to have a relaxed breakfast or brunch.

3 Restaurante El Encuentro
MAP L3 ■ c/San Vicente Mártir 28 ■ Closed Sun ■ www.restaurante elencuentro.es ■ €€

This intimate restaurant serves traditional Spanish food: hot and cold starters, market-fresh mains and a daily-changing rice dish.

4 Kaikaya
MAP L4 ■ Plaza del Ayuntamiento 10 ■ Closed Tue ■ www.kaikayarestaurante.com ■ €€

Japan meets Brazil at this tropical sushi place. Mix coconut shrimp with gyozas, and try the sangria made with sake.

5 El Poblet
MAP M4 ■ c/Correos 8 ■ Closed Tue & Sun ■ www.el pobletrestaurante.com ■ €€€

Part of super-chef Quique Dacosta's Valencian empire, this restaurant (with two Michelin stars) serves three sublime tasting menus that blend Spanish mainstays with unusual ingredients such as sea fennel.

6 Civera
MAP M4 ■ c/del Mosén Femades ■ 963 529 764 ■ €€

Smart, nautical-themed *marisquería* (seafood restaurant) where fresh dishes such as grilled rock fish and sea bass are ordered by weight.

7 Vuelve Carolina
MAP M4 ■ c/Correos 8 ■ www.vuelvecarolina.com ■ €€

Experience creative cooking from Quique Dacosta at this stylish place, where tapas include red-curry pork croquette and potato soufflé filled with liquid egg yolk.

Quique Dacosta's Vuelve Carolina

8 Café Madrid
MAP M3 ■ c/del Marqués de Dos Aguas ■ €€

Dishes are accompanied by a great cocktail menu at the hotel bar of Marqués House (see p130) but be sure to also try an Agua de Valencia.

9 Puerta del Mar
MAP L4 ■ c/Transits 4 ■ www. restaurantepuertadelmar.com ■ €€

Seafood is the focus here, but there are also meat and vegetarian options. The set lunch offers great value.

10 Secreto
MAP M3 ■ c/San Martín 11 ■ 627 756 946 ■ Closed Mon & Tue ■ €€

As suggested by the name, this spot is indeed a hidden gem. The passionate waiting staff know the ins and outs of every dish on the interesting menu.

See map on pp86–7

🔟 South of the Centro Histórico

The area south of the Centro Histórico only became part of Valencia when the city walls were torn down in 1868. L'Eixample (the Extension), a grid of tree-lined boulevards and grand buildings south of Calle Colón and the upmarket barrios (neighbourhoods) of El Pla del Remei and Gran Vía, known locally as Canovas, have attracted wealthy residents. Bohemian Ruzafa (Russafa in Valencian) to the southwest, with its cafés and independent boutiques, is gradually overtaking El Carmen as the city's hippest area. Bordering L'Eixample to the east is the Jardín del Turia. The gardens curl around the Centro Histórico to culminate in the spectacular Ciudad de las Artes y Ciencias, an iconic complex of buildings that is an unmissable sight.

A *fallas* statue, Museo Fallero

SOUTH OF THE CENTRO HISTÓRICO

1 **Top 10 Sights** see pp94–7

1 **Tapas Bars and Restaurants** see p101

1 **Shops** see p98

1 **Cafés** see p100

1 **Bars and Clubs** see p99

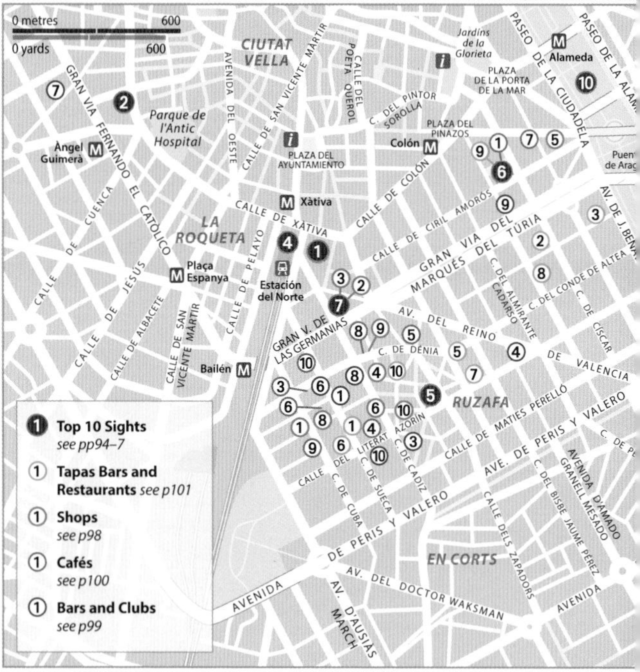

Preceding pages *The striking Art Deco façade of Casa Judía*

1 Plaza de Toros
MAP L5 ■ c/Xàtiva 28

Valencia's Neo-Classical bullring is one of the largest in Spain. It was built by Sebastián Monleón Estellés between 1850 and 1859 to a design that is clearly influenced by Rome's Colosseum. The bronze statue outside is of Manolo Montoliu, a Valencian *banderillero* (matador's assistant) who was killed by a bull in Seville in 1992. Fights unfortunately still take place – generally during Las Fallas and the Fería de Julio – but you can appreciate it as a building during one of the regular live concerts held here.

2 Teatre Micalet
MAP J4 ■ c/Guillem Castro 73 ■ www.teatremicalet.org

Housed in the Societat Coral El Micalet, a civic association founded in 1905, the Teatre Micalet has a distinguished tradition of staging musical performances and plays in the Valencian language. The intimate theatre has a varied and ever-changing programme, as the shows tend to run for just a few nights at a time.

3 Museo Fallero
MAP E5 ■ Plaza Monteolivete 4 ■ 962 084 625 ■ Adm; free Sun

In 1934, the influential local artist Regino Mas came up with an idea that forever changed the festival of Las Fallas. The public would vote on an Indult del Foc (Pardon from the Fire), which would save one *ninot* – papier-mâché figures that make up the *fallas* – from the flames of the final ceremony each year. Since then, the Museo Fallero has been collecting these winning *ninots* in an exhibition that now serves as a visual history of the festival's stylistic development.

Concourse of the Estación del Norte

4 Estación del Norte
MAP L5 ■ c/Xàtiva 24

Even if there is no train to catch, it is worth popping into the Estación del Norte. This grand station – located, despite its name, at the southern entrance to the Centro Histórico – is a Modernista delight, with a façade dotted with motifs and an interior of stained glass, iron and ceramics. There is also a tourist information desk, a handy left-luggage office, a little café-bar on platform 6 and a number of shops, including an outlet selling Valencia CF merchandise.

Stalls in Mercado de Ruzafa

5 Mercado de Ruzafa

MAP N6 ■ Plaza Barón de Cortes ■ Open 7am–3pm Mon–Sat ■ www.mercatderussafa.com

This neighbourhood market at the heart of Ruzafa was built in Brutalist concrete in 1957 by Julio Bellot Senet; its exterior was given a colourful makeover in 2007. Inside, there are all the usual stalls trading in meat, cheeses, flowers, fruit and vegetables. Check out Javi Algas, which sells seaweed.

6 Mercado de Colón

MAP N4 ■ c/Jorge Juan 19 ■ Open 7:30–2am Mon–Thu, 7:30–3am Fri–Sat ■ www.mercadocolon.es

It is hard to imagine today, but the dazzling Mercado de Colón was lying abandoned and in ruins at the turn of the 21st century. A complete renovation in 2003 restored the market to its former glory – with its wrought-iron roof, stained-glass windows, Gaudí-esque ornamentation and decorative mosaics, this is one of the city's finest Modernista buildings. The stalls of yesteryear have been replaced by cafés and tapas bars, and there is a food market on the floor below.

7 Casa Judía

MAP M5 ■ c/Castellón 20

The bold, colourful façade of Casa Judía (Jewish House), designed in Art Deco style by Valencian architect Joan Francisco Guardiola Martínez in 1930, is all the more striking for the way it pops out from its neighbours on Calle Castellón. Guardiola's trademark – combining elements from different cultures and countries – is evident in the building's blend of Egyptian, Arabic, Hindu and Eastern features. The Star of David on the lintel above the main entrance is the architect's nod to the original Jewish owner.

8 Museo Histórico Militar de Valencia

MAP E4 ■ c/General Gil Dolz 6 ■ 961 966 215 ■ Open 10am–2pm & 4–8pm Tue–Sat, 10am–2pm Sun

This well-organized military history museum charts the story of Spain's armed forces, with a focus on the Spanish Civil War. The permanent exhibition exceeds 2,000 pieces, comprising mostly flags, models, military clothing and weapons,

as well as a range of vehicles, including a tank, and some heavy artillery. Other exhibits touch on Valencia's relationship with the Spanish military and even the army's role in Las Fallas.

⑨ Ciudad de las Artes y Ciencias

Named one of the Twelve Treasures of Spain in 2017, alongside Gaudí's Sagrada Família in Barcelona and the Alhambra in Granada, the spectacular City of Arts and Sciences propelled Valencia into the limelight as a tourist destination. Designed mostly by Santiago Calatrava (Spanish-Mexican architect Félix Candela was responsible for the Oceanogràfic), this complex of sculptural structures includes an IMAX cinema and an interactive science museum *(see pp26–7)*.

⑩ Jardín del Turia

Curling around the top of the Centro Histórico and running down towards the sea, the Jardín del Turia *(see pp22–3)* is Valencia's green lung, a ribbon of parks and gardens where the Río Turia once flowed.

THE GREAT FLOOD OF VALENCIA

The Río Turia had already flooded some 75 times before it emphatically and devastatingly burst its banks on 14 October 1957, submerging large parts of the city. Known as La Gran Riada de Valencia (La Ruià in Valencian), the floods killed more than 80 people.

Mercado de Colón's imposing façade

A DAY AT THE CIUDAD DE LAS ARTES Y LAS CIENCIAS

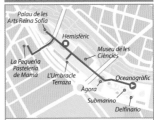

▶ MORNING

The first thing to do at the City of Arts and Sciences is nothing: just stand back and appreciate the size, beauty and architectural daring of these stunning Neo-Futurist buildings. Make a bee-line for **Oceanogràfic** *(see p26)* and head to the Temperate and Tropical aquariums to see Californian kelp forests and giant spider crabs from Japan. And keep an eye out for mauve stingers and sea nettles, part of the largest exhibit of jellyfish in Europe. Those without kids in tow might prefer a visit instead to the flagship **Palau de les Arts Reina Sofía** *(see p26)*. Informative guided tours take visitors around the opera house's various performance venues and include a visit to Plácido Domingo's Centro de Perfeccionamiento. Stop to eat at one of the many cafés or restaurants around the complex or cross Avenida Professor Lopez Piñero for lunch or a tasty treat at **La Pequeña Pastelería de Mamá** *(see p100)*.

AFTERNOON

Browse the hands-on exhibits at the **Museu de les Ciències** *(see p26)*. There is at least a couple of hours of entertainment here, learning about how chromosomes work and what zero gravity feels like. Wander through the sculpture garden in the Umbracle, stopping for a drink at the atmospheric **L'Umbracle Terraza** *(see p99)*, before catching a late-night screening at the **Hemisfèric** IMAX cinema *(see p27)*.

See map on pp94–5 ←

Shops

Stylish accessories in Gnomo

1 Gnomo
MAP L6 ▪ c/Cuba 32
▪ www.gnomo.eu

From fashion accessories to plant pots, this trendy lifestyle and design shop offers an eclectic selection of gifts. Look for work by contemporary Valencian artist Paula Bonet and illustrations by Laura Agustí.

2 El Vestidor Vintage
MAP M5 ▪ Gran Vía Germanías 14 ▪ www.elvestidorvintage.com

Stocking a consistently good range of vintage wear from brands such as Chanel and Dior, this boutique aims to give clothes a second chance.

3 Abanicos Carbonell
MAP M5 ▪ c/Castellón 21
▪ www.abanicoscarbonell.com

The Carbonells have been making traditional Spanish fans by hand since 1810. The shelves are piled high with beautiful fans, ranging in price from €2 up to €12,000.

4 Lacontra
MAP M6 ▪ c/Cádiz 38
▪ www.lacontraroom.com

With its own clothing line, this boutique also offers a carefully curated selection of labels, including Samsøe Samsøe and Nudie Jeans. The emphasis is on ethical and sustainable fashion.

5 Mantequerías Vicente Ferrero
MAP P4 ▪ c/Sorní 38 ▪ 963 749 724

The service is friendly at this traditional neighbourhood grocery. Taste the cheeses and Iberian hams before eating in or taking away.

6 Librería Bartleby
MAP M6 ▪ c/Cádiz 50
▪ 963 237 184

This independent bookstore sells a winning combination of books, comics and wines. There is a good range of cultural events, too, from talks and recitals to live music.

7 Ana Illueca
MAP G5 ▪ Rodrigo de Pertegás 42 ▪ www.anaillueca.com

Master potter Illeuca uses methods developed by the Moors to create concept works for her ceramics store.

8 Madame Mim
MAP M6 ▪ c/Puerto Rico 30
▪ 963 255 941

One of the best thrift stores in Ruzafa, Madame Mim is a trove of vintage goodies: clothes (to rent or to buy), antique items and other knick-knacks.

9 Kowalski Cosas Bellas Artes
MAP M6 ▪ c/Denia 20 ▪ www.kowalskicosasbellasartes.com

In addition to drawing and painting materials, there is also a collection of books, felt hats, leather jackets, shoes and vinyl records here.

10 Müza
MAP D5 ▪ c/Reina Na Maria 5

A tea shop, with lovely owners and a wide variety of delicious teas, Müza also has pretty teapots and some heavenly scented candles available to purchase.

Bars and Clubs

1 Olhöps Craft Beer House
MAP M6 ■ c/Sueca 21
■ www.olhops.com

Ten craft beers on tap complement the more than 100 bottled beers available here. Try their own H2ÖL ales or ice cream made with beer (the vanilla is made with stout, the chocolate with porter). Another Ruzafa outlet, Olhöps Craft Beer Lab, is on Calle Carlos Cervera.

2 L'Umbracle Terraza
MAP F6 ■ Av del Professor López Piñero 5 ■ www.umbracle terraza.com

There are great views over the City of Arts and Sciences from this terrace bar under the arches of the Umbracle. Tables are dotted among lush foliage for alfresco drinks. Join the young crowd below ground at Mya, where DJs play until late *(see p27)*.

3 La Madriguera
MAP M6 ■ c/Cádiz 70

Expertly prepared cocktails, friendly staff and excellent service have made this one of the most popular night spots in trendy Ruzafa.

4 Ruzanuvol
MAP N5 ■ c/Lluís de Santàngel
■ www.ruzanuvol.com

The friendly staff at this brewery will help pair your pint with something from the menu of dishes made with fresh market produce.

5 Wah Wah
MAP G5 ■ c/Campoamor 52
■ www.wahwahclub.es

This intimate live music club has an impressive track record of attracting top international indie bands.

6 Bar Vermúdez
MAP M6 ■ c/Sueca 16
■ 963 034 774

Always buzzing with locals, Vermúdez is a friendly bar with a long list of vermouths – a fortified Spanish wine flavoured with herbs; order a *vermut casero* (house vermouth) with tapas and take it outside for people-watching on this busy Ruzafa street.

7 Loco Club
MAP J4 ■ c/Erudito Orellana 12
■ www.lococlub.es

New acts are given the stage one night a month at this long-standing, atmospheric club with live music – mostly rock, pop and indie – but also occasionally country and soul.

8 La Fusteria
MAP M6 ■ c/Cádiz 28
■ 963 935 653

Once a carpenter's workshop, this laid-back bar is a good early evening spot to enjoy a ZETA craft beer.

9 Aquarium
MAP N5 ■ c/Gran Via de Marqués del Túria 57 ■ 963 510 040

Going strong since 1957, this classic bar has dapper staff who take real care with their craft, delivering perfect drinks to a mostly local clientele.

10 Ubik Café
MAP L6 ■ c/Literato Azorín 13
■ 963 741 255

Relax with a coffee or a beer, while away the afternoon over a board game or catch a gig at this popular bookshop café in Ruzafa.

The bar in Ubik Café

See map on pp94–5

Cafés

1 Casa Orxata
MAP N4 ■ Mercado de Colón
■ 963 527 307

This all-day *horchatería* is on the ground floor of the striking Mercado de Colón. Order an organic *horchata*, served here without sugar, or a freshly squeezed Valencia orange juice and soak up the surroundings.

The Casa Orxata stall

2 La Pequeña Pastelería de Mamá
MAP F6 ■ c/Poeta Josep Cervera y Grifol 14 ■ 963 444 495

Cute and very homely, this pastry shop makes the perfect spot for brunch or an afternoon treat of tea and cakes, and is located close to the Ciudad de las Artes y Ciencias.

3 Café ArtySana
MAP M6 ■ c/Denia 49
■ 697 280 999 ■ Closed Mon

A good range of homemade vegan and vegetarian food is served at this hipster café and art space. Go for the terrific *tostadas* and detox drinks. The courtyard is a real oasis.

4 La Cantina de Ruzafa
MAP L6 ■ c/Literato Azorín 13

Try the classic Valencian breakfast, *esmorzaret*, here. It starts with olives, pickled peppers, peanuts and beans, followed by a chunky roll, and ends with a *cremaet* (coffee with a shot of rum).

5 Buñolería Churrería el Contraste
MAP M6 ■ c/San Valero 12
■ 963 734 611 ■ Closed Sat & Sun

Many locals swear by the deep-fried goodies – *buñuelos*, *churros* and the shorter, fatter *purros* – served up at this family-run café.

6 Bluebell Coffee Roasters
MAP L6 ■ c/Buenos Aires 3 ■ 963 225 413 ■ www.bluebellcoffeeco.com

A serious coffee shop that roasts its own speciality coffees, Bluebell serves light meals as well. There are occasional tastings and workshops, too.

7 La Petite Brioche Sorní
MAP P4 ■ c/Sorní 28
■ 963 223 677 ■ Closed Sun & Mon

There is a delicious selection of sweet and savoury treats at this lovely bakery – brownies, pancakes and homemade cakes.

8 Slaughterhouse
MAP M6 ■ c/Denia 22
■ 960 223 820 ■ Closed Sun & Mon

This evening-only bookshop café, set in a former butcher's shop, is famous for its artisan burgers. This being Ruzafa, there are also plenty of exhibitions and live music events.

9 Dulce de Leche
MAP L6 ■ c/Pintor Gisbert 2
■ 960 035 949

Everything tastes as good as it looks at this Ruzafa outpost of the citywide Argentinian bakery. It is especially hard to resist anything that is drizzled in the namesake caramel sauce.

10 Pastelería Limón y Merengue
MAP L6 ■ c/Sueca 6 ■ Closed Tue
■ www.pastelerialimonymerengue.es

Located on the northern fringes of Ruzafa, this *pastelería* has forged a reputation as one of the best in the city. Cakes like "Snow White" and "Dolce Vita" are works of art.

Tapas Bars and Restaurants

PRICE CATEGORIES

For a three-course meal for one with half a bottle of wine (or equivalent meal), taxes and extra charges.

€ under €35   €€ €35–60   €€€ over €60

1 El Rodamón de Russafa
MAP D5 ■ c/Sueca 47
■ 963 218 014 ■ €€

Globetrotting tapas in a formal but fun environment – the "Mowgli vs Shere Khan" section on the menu includes curried calamari, while "God Save the Queen" features miniature portions of sausage and mash.

2 Racó de Turia
MAP N5 ■ c/Císcar 10
■ 963 951 525 ■ €€

This is one of the best places in the city to try paella or other local dishes, such as *all i pebre* (eel stew) and *fideuà* (paella with noodles).

3 Restaurante Gordon 10
MAP N5 ■ c/Conde Altea 49
■ 963 740 787 ■ Closed Mon ■ €€

The steaks at this Argentinian *parrilla* are paraded in front of you so you can choose your favoured cut.

4 PULPO
MAP E5 ■ c/Chile 5 ■ 963 811 266 ■ Closed Mon & Tue ■ €€

The menu changes weekly at PULPO, depending on what's in season, but octopus and cuttlefish are always favourites.

5 Canalla Bistro
MAP N6 ■ c/Maestro José Serrano 5 ■ 963 740 509 ■ €€

Ricard Camerena's stylish bistro offers a good menu of international dishes, from courgette flower tempura to a New York Reuben sandwich.

6 La Cooperativa del Mar
MAP D5 ■ c/Literato Azorín 18
■ 963 224 442 ■ €

The tinned seafood stacked behind the marble counter, mostly from Portugal, forms the basis of the menu here. Try the spicy tomato mackerel, with a glass of vinho verde.

7 Nozomi Sushi Bar
MAP N6 ■ c/Pedro III El Grande 11 ■ 961 487 764 ■ Closed Mon, Tue & Sun ■ €€

The attention to detail in the decor is matched by the quality of the tasting menus at this sushi spot.

8 Mercatbar
MAP N5 ■ c/Joaquín Costa 27
■ 963 748 558 ■ Closed Sun ■ €€

Quique Dacosta's first restaurant in Valencia serves delicious tapas – the most affordable way of enjoying the great chef's creative cuisine.

9 Ma Khin Café
MAP N4 ■ Mercado del Colon, c/Jorge Juan 19 ■ www.makhincafe.com ■ €€

Take a culinary tour around South East Asia at this stylish spot in the Mercado del Colon. The range of flavours, beautifully presented dishes and attentive service make this a local favourite.

The kitchen of Fierro

10 Fierro
MAP M6 ■ c/Doctor Serrano 4
■ 963 305 244 ■ Open D Thu, Fri & Sat by prior reservation only ■ €€€

This Michelin-starred restaurant has just four tables where a handful of guests are served extraordinary dishes from a tasting menu by chefs Carito Lourenço and Germán Carrizo.

See map on pp94–5

🔟 North of the Centro Histórico

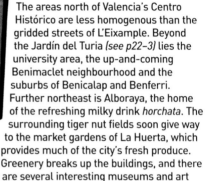

The areas north of Valencia's Centro Histórico are less homogenous than the gridded streets of L'Eixample. Beyond the Jardín del Turia (see p22–3) lies the university area, the up-and-coming Benimaclet neighbourhood and the suburbs of Benicalap and Benferri. Further northeast is Alboraya, the home of the refreshing milky drink horchata. The surrounding tiger nut fields soon give way to the market gardens of La Huerta, which provides much of the city's fresh produce. Greenery breaks up the buildings, and there are several interesting museums and art galleries, most notably the Museo de Bellas Artes. The sights here are more widespread but still easily accessible – none are more than a 20-minute walk from the nearest metro station.

Triptych, Museo de la Historia de Valencia

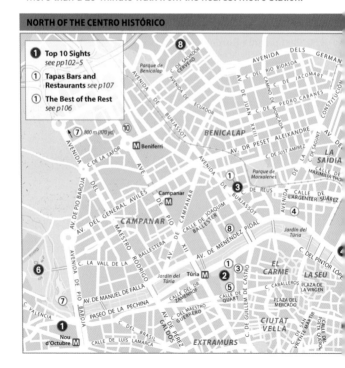

NORTH OF THE CENTRO HISTÓRICO

① Top 10 Sights
see pp102–5

① Tapas Bars and Restaurants see p107

① The Best of the Rest
see p106

1 Museo de Historia de Valencia

MAP B4 ■ c/Valencia 42 ■ Open 10am–7pm Tue–Sat, 10am–2pm Sun ■ Adm ■ https://mhv.valencia.es

Located in a 19th-century water cistern, this museum charts Valencia's eventful history, from its founding as a Roman city and Muslim *taifa* (principality) to life under Franco. Scientific instruments, archaeological objects, books and costumes are displayed among the atmospherically lit brick columns, with each era brought to life with a multimedia display.

2 Jardín Botánico

MAP C4 ■ c/Quart 80 ■ Open Mar & Oct: 10am–7pm; May–Aug: 10am–9pm; Sep: 10am–8pm; Nov & Dec: 10am–6pm ■ Adm ■ www.jardibotanic.org

The University of Valencia's botanical gardens extend for 4 ha (10 acres) just west of the Centro Histórico, providing a lovely respite from the city's busy streets. The gardens were founded in 1567, although they did not move to their current location until the early 19th century. After falling into disrepair the gardens were renovated and reopened in 1991. Highlights include orchids, bromeliads and palms, carnivorous plants and species that have adapted to grow in desert climates.

3 Bombas Gens Centre d'Art

MAP C3 ■ Avda Burjassot 54 ■ Open 4–8pm Wed, 11am–2pm & 4–8pm Thu–Sun; guided tours in English at 5pm (book in advance) ■ www.bombasgens.com

The Art Deco Bombas Gens is a good example of Valencia's ongoing regeneration. Originally a 1930s hydraulic pump factory, the structure lay abandoned until 2014, when it was converted into a superb gallery of contemporary art and photography. The free guided tours, which are led by enthusiastic experts, are well worth reserving in advance.

4 Museo de Bellas Artes

The Museum of Fine Arts holds one of Spain's best collections of paintings dating from the 15th to the 19th centuries. It is best known for works by Joaquín Sorolla and Primitive Valencian painters such as Joan Reixach, Nicolau Falcó and Joan de Joanes, but there are some very impressive Renaissance works here too *(see pp30–33)*.

Gallery in the Museo de Bellas Artes

Strolling among the trees in the verdant Jardines del Real

⑤ Jardines del Real
MAP E3 ■ c/San Pío V ■ Open Apr–Oct: 7:30am–9:30pm daily; Nov–Mar: 7:30am–8:30pm Mon–Fri, 7:30am–9:30pm Sat & Sun

These picturesque gardens make for a welcome sanctuary from the Centro Histórico bustle. Among the rosebeds and tree-lined paths is some fine statuary, including the *Four Seasons* carved by the Genoese sculptor Jacobo Antonio Ponzanelli. The gardens take their name from the palace that was built here in the 11th century as a retreat for the Muslim king Abd al-Aziz; extended by King Jaume I and rebuilt by Pedro IV, it was destroyed by Spanish troops during the War of Independence.

⑥ BIOPARC
MAP A3 ■ Avda Pío Baroja ■ Adm; under 4s free ■ www.bioparc valencia.es

This brilliant African wildlife park has been thoughtfully designed to use rivers, trees and ditches rather than cages to enclose the animals, with kopjes, baobabs and waterfalls helping to create a realistic natural environment. It's easy to spend a few hours here, discovering the different species and attending a couple of the activities, such as the elephant feeding.

A Hartlaub's turaco perching in BIOPARC

⑦ Museo de Ciencias Naturales
MAP E3 ■ c/General Élio 9 ■ 962 084 313 ■ Open 10am–5pm Tue–Fri, 10am–8pm Sat & Sun ■ Adm ■ www.mncn.csic.es

Located in the middle of the Jardines del Real in a former Rationalist building, the Natural History Museum is an eclectic showcase of exhibits, ranging from a collection of molluscs to displays on the region's incredibly varied biodiversity. The star of the show is the collection of Pleistocene fossils discovered in South America by a Valencian engineer. The mammal skeletons, referenced in naturalist Charles Darwin's *On the Origin of Species*, include a sabre-toothed tiger and a Megatherium, a giant ground sloth the size of an elephant.

⑧ Museo del Gremio de Artistas Falleros
MAP C1 ■ Avda San José Artesano 15 ■ Open 10am–2pm & 4–7pm Mon–Fri, 10am–2pm Sat; closed Aug ■ Adm ■ www.gremiodeartistasfalleros.es

The Gremio de Artistas Falleros (Guild of Fallas Artists) was founded in 1943 by Regino Mas. He was instrumental in a number of Fallas milestones, instigating the Indult del Foc *(p34)* and pushing for the creation of the Ciudad Fallera, a neighbourhood of workshops and warehouses. This "city" is now home to the guild's museum, which details all the stages involved in making these monuments, from initial sketches to final *falla*.

⑨ Monasterio de San Miguel de los Reyes

MAP D1 ■ Avda de la Constitución 284 ■ Open 9am–8pm Mon–Fri, 9am–1:30pm Sat; guided visits: noon (Valencian) & 1pm (Spanish) Sat & Sun ■ www.bv.gva.es

Fernando de Aragon, the Duke of Calabria, founded this monastery in 1546, enlisting the services of the architects Alonso de Covarrubias and Juan de Vidaña for its design. Considered one of the finest examples of the Valencian Renaissance, the impressive complex has housed the Valencian Library since 1999.

Monasterio de San Miguel de los Reyes

⑩ La Mestalla

MAP E4 ■ Avda de Suecia ■ Adm ■ www.valenciacf.com

This stadium has been the home of Valencia Club de Fútbol, the city's top team, since 1923. Regular guided tours visit the home team's dressing room and take visitors through the players' tunnel and on to the pitch. The best way to appreciate it, though, is to see a match, when nearly 50,000 supporters pack into its stands.

LO RAT PENAT

A bat with outstretched wings, Lo Rat Penat is the symbol of Valencia, cropping up on the city's coat of arms and the crest of Valencia Club de Fútbol. Legend has it that while Jaume I was camped outside Valencia in 1238, a bat nested atop his tent. The king ordered the nest be left alone; the bat repaid him by sabotaging a Moorish attack, thus earning its place in heraldic history.

A CYCLE ROUND THE PERIFERÍCO NORTE

▶ MORNING

Pick up a set of wheels from Valencia Bikes *(see p125)* and cycle through the **Jardín del Turia** *(see pp22–3)*, crossing the colourful Puente de Flores en route to the Modernist Palacio de la Exposicion, built by Francisco Mora Berenguer in 1909. Head up Avenida de Suecia, in the shadow of mighty **La Mestalla** football stadium, and merge onto the cycle lanes of the Periferíco Norte, which arcs around the city's northern suburbs; the Jenga-like building to the left here is the **Espai Verd** *(see p59)*.

Stop for a refreshing *horchata* drink at **Horchatería Daniel** *(see p106)* in Alboraya before carrying on along the ring road to the **Monasterio de San Miguel de los Reyes**. It is 2.5 km (2 miles) from here to the **Museo del Gremio de Artistas Falleros**; explore the museum, then grab lunch at the restaurant next door.

AFTERNOON

Spend the afternoon splashing about in the nearby **Piscina Parque Benicalap** *(see p61)* before starting the journey back towards the Centro Histórico. Cycle by the Palacio de Congresos *(Avda Cortes Velencianas)*, a convention centre designed by Norman Foster, and down the Avenida de las Cortes Valencianas to Manolo Valdés's *Iberian Lady*, made from thousands of pieces of blue-glazed ceramics. A detour right along Calle de la Safor will lead through **Parque de Cabecera** *(see p106)*; otherwise, keep heading south to end up back at the bike rental shop.

See map on pp102–3 ◀

The Best of the Rest

Façade of the Teatro La Estrella

1 Teatro la Estrella
MAP J2 ▪ c/Dr Sanchez Bergón 29 ▪ Adm ▪ www.teatro laestrella.com

The fairy tale shows at this engaging puppet theatre provide an hour of good old-fashioned children's entertainment. There is a sister venue down by the waterfront in El Cabanyal.

2 Bodega Baltasar Segui
MAP E2 ▪ c/Emilio Baró 17

This traditional winery in the Benimaclet neighbourhood stocks a great selection of Valencian and Spanish wines and vermouths.

3 Café del Duende
MAP J1 ▪ c/Turia 62
▪ www.cafedelduende.com

The traditional flamenco shows at this appealingly low-key small venue are deservedly popular.

4 Lladró
MAP M4 ▪ Ctra de Alboraya, Tavernes Blanques ▪ Open 10am–6pm Mon–Fri, 10am–2pm Sat ▪ www.lladro.com

Even if Lladró's porcelain figurines seem too expensive to buy, it is still worth visiting their headquarters for a (free) guided tour.

5 Vinyl Eye
MAP J2 ▪ c/Turia 35

The boutique of this music-influenced clothing brand is part art gallery, part T-shirt shop. Unique designs include the works of Valencian street artists.

6 Black Note Club
MAP E4 ▪ c/Polo y Peyrolón 15

This atmospheric venue is one of the best places in Valencia to hear live music, whether it is rock, soul, R&B or blues.

7 Parque de Cabecera
MAP B4 ▪ Avda Pío Baroja

Located at the northern end of the Jardín del Turia (cabecera means "entrance"), this park has been designed to mirror the landscape of the river that originally flowed here.

8 Dulzumat
MAP C3 ▪ Avda Menéndez Pidal 8 ▪ 963 402 620 ▪ €

This long-running pastelería (pastry shop) draws locals from far and wide with its delectable handmade cakes, chocolates and other treats.

9 Horchatería Daniel
MAP E3 ▪ Avda de la Horchata 41 ▪ 961 858 866 ▪ €

Daniel Tortajada started selling horchata from his house in 1960. Today, the horchatería he later set up sells 140,000 litres of this nutty milk drink every year, along with a million fartons, the long, sweet pastry finger that he invented.

10 Jardín de Monforte
MAP C3 ▪ Plaza de la Legión Española ▪ Open 10am–8pm daily (to 6pm autumn & winter)

One of the most beautiful gardens in the city, the Jardín de Monforte was designed by the Valencian architect Sebastián Monleón Estellés, who split it into two areas – a Romantic Garden and a Geometric Garden.

Statues in the Jardín de Monforte

Tapas Bars and Restaurants

PRICE CATEGORIES

For a three-course meal for one with half a bottle of wine (or equivalent meal), taxes and extra charges.

€ under €35 €€ €35–60 €€€ over €60

1 Ricard Camarena Restaurant

MAP C3 ▪ Avda de Burjassot 54 ▪ Closed Mon & Tue ▪ https://ricard camarena.com ▪ €€€

Located in the Bombas Gens Centre d'Art *(p103)*, the flagship restaurant of Ricard Camarena's Valencian empire is experiential dining at its best.

2 Olegari

MAP F3 ▪ c/Músico Hipólito Martínez 8 ▪ 960 623 787 ▪ €

This simple pizzeria takes the hassle out of ordering – you decide how many slices you want and the toppings are chosen for you.

3 Tanto Monta

MAP F3 ▪ c/Poeta Artola 19 ▪ 963 298 106 ▪ Closed Sun ▪ €

Select from a tempting array of hearty *montaditos* (little sandwiches) and varied *pinchos* (Basque tapas).

4 Joaquín Schmidt

MAP D3 ▪ c/Visitación 7 ▪ 963 401 710 ▪ Closed Sun ▪ €€€

The eponymous chef cooks and serves a four-, five- or seven-course menu completely of his choosing at this unusual but enjoyable restaurant.

5 El Rinconet

MAP E3 ▪ Plaza Polo de Bernabe 4 ▪ 963 819 335 ▪ Closed Sun ▪ €

This welcoming Spanish restaurant has made a name for itself with its hearty, flavourful dishes.

6 Balansiya

MAP F3 ▪ Paseo de las Facultades 3 ▪ 963 890 824 ▪ €€

It is well worth making the journey up to Tarongers for this Moroccan restaurant, whose tagines and couscous dishes evoke the flavours of Al-Andalus. It is hard to miss the entrance, with its Mudéjar-style arch and tiled fountain.

7 Tavella Restaurant

MAP B2 ▪ Camino Viejo de Líria 93 ▪ Closed Mon & Sun ▪ www.tavella restaurant.com ▪ €€

Pablo Chirivella's restaurant offers high-class cooking with a focus on the finest and freshest ingredients. The dishes are packed full of produce from the Mediterranean Sea and the nearby fields of La Huerta.

Tavella Restaurant

8 El Aprendiz

MAP E3 ▪ Plaza Río Duero 6 ▪ Closed Mon ▪ www.elaprendiz tapas.com ▪ €€

This stylishly stripped-back spot serves a globetrotting range of fusion tapas.

9 Lienzo

MAP N2 ▪ Plaza Tetúan 18 ▪ Closed Mon ▪ www.restaurante lienzo.com ▪ €€

The minimalist interior is the perfect backdrop for a meal of stylish gastro-tapas at this classy restaurant.

10 Voltereta

MAP N5 ▪ Avda de las Cortes Valencianas 26 ▪ 962 604 607 ▪ €€

The modern fusion tapas here are served in an unusual setting with lamps dangling from large trees – it feels like the dining room is outside.

See map on pp102–3

🔟 The Seafront

First settled in the 13th century, the fishing districts along the Mediterranean, collectively known today as the Poblats Marítims, developed separately from the city. As recently as 1897, El Cabanyal – the term for the three neighbourhoods (Canyamelar, Cap de França and El Cabanyal itself) that extend north from the port – was an independent municipality. This faded fishing quarter is an atmospheric area to explore, its eclectic houses covered with tiles in maritime hues of blue, white and green. Most people, though, are drawn here by the beaches, some of the best in Spain, which are backed for the most part by a promenade of seafood restaurants.

Bust of Blasco Ibanez at the Casa-Museo Blasco Ibañez

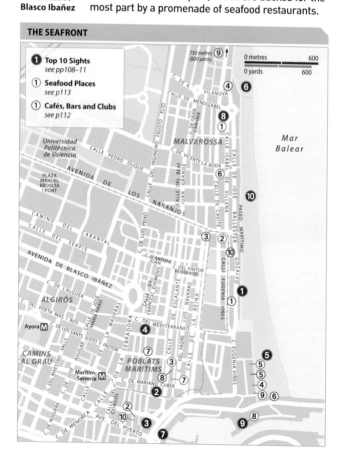

THE SEAFRONT

Top 10 Sights
see pp108–11

Seafood Places
see p113

Cafés, Bars and Clubs
see p112

Walkers and cyclists sharing the seafront Paseo Marítimo

① Paseo Marítimo
MAP H4

Lined by rows of palm trees, the Paseo Marítimo runs for 2.5 km (2 miles) behind Playa de las Arenas and Playa de la Malvarossa. It starts at the giant flags near the marina and leads all the way north to the roundabout that effectively marks the border between Malvarossa and Playa de la Patacona. The beach-hugging promenade is shadowed by a cycle lane its entire length. Visit in the evening, when locals turn out for a stroll with their families.

② Museo del Arroz
MAP G5 ■ c/del Rosario 3 ■ 963 525 478 ■ Open 10am–2pm & 3–7pm Tue–Sat, 10am–2pm Sun ■ Adm

One of the city's major exports and a fundamental ingredient in many of the region's traditional dishes, rice continues to play an important role in Valencian life. Located in a former 1900s rice mill, the Molino de Serra, this museum is full of restored machinery from the turn of the 20th century and charts the grain's journey from rice field to rice sack.

③ Atarazanas del Grao
MAP G5 ■ Plaza Juan Antonio Benlliure ■ 963 525 478 ■ Open 10am–2pm & 3–7pm Tue–Sat, 10am–3pm Sun ■ Adm

These five 14th-century warehouses were used to build and repair boats during the heyday of Valencia's international maritime trade. They were beautifully restored during the 1990s and now house occasional temporary exhibitions.

④ Mercado del Cabanyal
MAP G5 ■ c/Martí Grajales 4 ■ Open 7am–2:30pm Mon–Sat ■ www.mercadocabanyal.es

The people of El Cabanyal used to shop at various neighbourhood street markets in Canyamelar, Cap de França and El Cabanyal until the construction of the large, pink Mercado del Cabanyal in 1958. Ever since, the market has been a popular place for fresh meat, fruit and vegetables, plus superb seafood hauled off boats at the nearby beaches. It is best to visit in the early morning when the market is a hive of activity.

Fresh produce, Mercado del Cabanyal

5 Playa de las Arenas
MAP H5

The start of Valencia's long stretch of fantastic beaches, and the closest to the marina, Playa de las Arenas is easily reached by tram from Marítim-Serrería metro station. There are sunloungers and thatched sunshades for rent, and a lifeguard is on duty in the summer. The restaurants along Paseo Marítimo here back onto the leafy Paseo de Neptuno and offer the best choice of beachfront dining. The northern half of Arenas is also known as Playa del Cabanyal, after the nearby neighbourhood.

6 Playa de la Patacona
MAP H2

The northernmost, and quietest, city beach, Playa de la Patacona fronts the Alboraya neighbourhood and runs north for 2 km (1 mile) to the Río Carraixet. In summer, grab a drink and some shade at a wooden *chiringuito* (beach bar); La Más Bonita Chiringuito is the most appealing, set in front of La Más Bonita Patacona café *(see p112)*, but there are plenty of other lower-key options.

7 Edificio del Reloj
MAP G5 ■ Muelle del Grao ■ Open 10:30am–5pm daily

Designed by Federico de Membrillera, this Neo-Classical building is named after the *reloj* (clock) in the top

The Veles e Vents pavilion

of its tower. Built in 1916, it was once a ticket and customs office and is now the Port Authority headquarters.

8 Casa-Museo Blasco Ibañez
MAP H3 ■ c/Isabel de Villena 159 ■ Open 10am–2pm & 3–7pm Tue–Sat & 10am–2pm Sun ■ Adm ■ www.casamuseoblascoibanez.com

The journalist and novelist Vicente Blasco Ibañez (1867–1928) wrote about life in La Huerta *(see p118)*, most notably in *Cañas y Barro (Reeds and Mud)*. Outside Spain he is best known for his later works that were made into films – the Hollywood adaptation of *Four Horseman of the Apocalypse* launched the career of actor Rudolfo Valentino. This museum, built on the site of Ibañez's original villa and featuring a near-identical façade, explores the writer's personal life and contains some of his prized possessions, such as his pipe, glasses, travel journals and furniture from his office at *El Pueblo* newspaper.

9 Veles e Vents
MAP H5 ■ Muelle de la Aduana

This sleek ultramodern building was the centrepiece of the project to regenerate Valencia's port ahead of the America's Cup in 2007. The pavilion, made up of white concrete

Edificio del Reloj clocktower

horizontal platforms, is a dramatic addition to the waterfront's skyline, although its design owes much to the time limits faced by British architect David Chipperfield, who had just 11 months to deliver the project after winning the commission. The building is named after a 15th-century poem by Ausiàs March (see p49), and houses several restaurants, including La Sucursal (see p113).

THE AMERICA'S CUP IN VALENCIA

Valencia has twice hosted the world's most prestigious sailing event. When defending Swiss champions Alinghi were unable to stage the 2007 event in their landlocked country, Valencia won the hosting rights – an opportunity the city authorities used to revamp the port, creating the Juan Carlos I Marina and the Veles e Vents. When Alinghi won again in 2007, Valencia staged its second America's Cup three years later.

⑩ Playa de la Malvarossa
MAP H3

Linking Playa de las Arenas in the south and Playa de la Patacona in the north, the sweeping Playa de la Malvarossa is the most popular of the city beaches. There is usually a good mix of couples, families and groups of friends enjoying some of the excellent sports facilities – basketball nets and football goals, along with a beach volleyball centre.

AN AFTERNOON TOUR OF EL CABANYAL'S TILED HOUSES

⊳ Start your exploration of this charming fishing quarter in the **Mercado del Cabanyal** (see p109), stocking up on provisions to tide any hunger over until dinner. Then walk down Calle de Mediterráneo until you get to No 37. The mosaic on the house here, also known as the Casa del Oso, depicts *pesca dels bous*, an old Cabanyal method of trawling in which oxen were used to pull the fishing boats ashore; it is a scene that appears in several of Joaquín Sorrolla's most famous paintings, including *The Return from Fishing* and *Afternoon Sun*. Backtrack a few yards and turn right onto Calle de la Reina, where there are some fabulous examples of El Cabanyal's decorative ceramics at No 164, No 173 and No 180. Take the next left and follow the road to Calle de Escalante. The harmonious block of green-and-white chequerboard houses at No 225 is one of the prettiest examples in the neighbourhood.

Retrace your steps back towards Calle de la Reina and turn left onto Calle del Progreso, where No 262 and No 279 are virtually opposite each other, both feature vase mosaics and griffin-head drains. Keep heading north, then turn left onto Calle Don Vicente Guillot and first right onto Calle de José Benlliure. The row of green-and-white checkerboard houses at Nos 315–317 were built in 1928 and are topped by an impressive balustrade and a lovely broken-tile vase trencadís. For dinner, head towards the beach and enjoy fresh fish at ⊐ **La Lonja del Pescado** (see p113).

See map on p108

Cafés, Bars and Clubs

The plant-adorned La Fábrica de Hielo

1 La Fábrica de Hielo
MAP H5 ▪ c/Pavia 37
▪ 963 682 619 ▪ Closed Mon

Tuck into a focaccia sandwich or a Galician burger from La Regional's mobile street-food truck while listening to funk jam sessions or bluegrass at this shabby chic cultural centre occupying an old ice factory just off Playa de las Arenas.

2 Bodega La Peseta
MAP G5 ▪ c/del Cristo del Grao 16 ▪ 960 431 585

This backstreet winery is always busy with locals snacking on tapas in between meals or spilling out onto the pavement with a vermouth.

3 Bodega La Pascuala
MAP H4 ▪ c/Dr Lluch 299
▪ 963 713 814

Established over a century ago, this popular, bare-bones bodega makes enormous sandwiches with hearty fillings that are big enough to feed a family.

4 La Más Bonita Patacona
MAP H4 ▪ Paseo Marítimo de la Patacona 11 ▪ 961 143 611

With its whitewashed walls, turquoise shutters and cacti-filled planters, this cool café on the beach-front in Alboroya has an island feel. Come for brunch, then return in the evening for cocktails.

5 Destino 56
MAP H5
▪ Paseo Neptuno 56
▪ 963 724 433

There is a lounge-bar vibe at this restaurant on Las Arenas's palm tree-lined esplanade. It's a good place for an evening drink, with over a dozen gins.

6 Marina Beach Club
MAP H5 ▪ c/Marina Real Juan Carlos I ▪ www.marinabeachclub.com

The trendiest spot on the waterfront, this is a see-and-be-seen kind of place. The day beds are pricey but the pool is fantastic and the complex is open until the early hours.

7 Anyora
MAP G5 ▪ c/Don Vicente Gallart 15 ▪ 963 558 809

Enjoy a glass or two of natural wine at the welcoming bar, perched beneath hanging herbs, at this stylish tiled winery.

8 Botadura Coctelería
MAP G5 ▪ c/Josep Benlliure 27

This bar serves great cocktails. The bartenders will shake up something special for you if you tell them what you're in the mood to drink.

9 Chirringuito Elocho
MAP H4 ▪ Paseo Marítimo de la Patacona 93 ▪ 634 839 961

Thatched roofs provide plenty of shade for a cold beer or Agua de Valencia at this laid-back, low-key beach bar on Playa de la Patacona.

10 Akuarela Playa
MAP H3 ▪ c/Eugenia Viñes 152
▪ 963 374 720

This multispace night club on the Playa de la Malvarossa beachfront offers plenty of musical choice. Note that it only really gets going at 3am.

Seafood Places

PRICE CATEGORIES

For a three-course meal for one with half a bottle of wine (or equivalent meal), taxes and extra charges.

€ under €35   €€ €35–60   €€€ over €60

1 Casa Carmela
MAP H3 ▪ c/Isabel de Villena 155 ▪ 963 710 073 ▪ Closed Mon ▪ €€

Consistently excellent paellas and rice dishes are the order of the day at this smart restaurant near the northern tip of Playa de la Malvarossa.

2 La Lonja del Pescado
MAP H4 ▪ c/Eugenia Viñes 243 ▪ 963 553 535 ▪ Closed Mon ▪ €

It's worth leaving the seafront for this no-frills traditional restaurant, housed in the old El Cabanyal fish market, which focuses its efforts on cooking really good fresh seafood.

3 Casa Montaña
MAP G5 ▪ c/de José Benlliure 69 ▪ 963 672 314 ▪ €€

Pull up a stool in the front room, where the walls are lined with dark, towering wine barrels, or duck under the bar for a quieter meal out back. Either way, this atmospheric *taberna* offers a medley of superb tapas.

4 Bar Cabanyal
MAP G4 ▪ c/Martí Grajales 5 ▪ 961 335 377 ▪ Closed Mon ▪ €

This low-key restaurant, with pretty turquoise-and-white décor, serves super-fresh seafood tapas and bigger dishes such as grilled octopus and crab salad in its shell. It offers fresh food and great value for money.

5 La Paz
MAP H5 ▪ Paseo Neptuno 68 ▪ 963 561 983 ▪ www.lapazvalencia.com ▪ €€

A top choice on Playa Arenas's restaurant-laden beachfront, La Paz offers starters such as clams and cuttlefish, followed by paella or lightly grilled seafood.

6 Casa Cesar
MAP H3 ▪ c/Isabel de Villena 71 ▪ 963 555 710 ▪ €€

Great rice dishes are served here, and everything, from whole grilled squid to salted-cod *esgarrat* (see p65), is fresh from the sea.

7 Casa Guillermo
MAP G5 ▪ c/del Progreso 15 ▪ 963 179 177 ▪ Closed Sun ▪ €€

It's difficult to look beyond the signature anchovies at this tapas bar, but try other dishes, such as *titaina*, a speciality with tomatoes and tuna.

8 La Sucursal
MAP H5 ▪ Veles e Vents, Muelle de la Aduana ▪ 645 201 679 ▪ Closed Mon ▪ €€€

Expect tasting menus and excellent service at this Michelin-starred spot on the top floor of the Veles e Vents building, with tremendous views.

9 La Pepica
MAP H5 ▪ Paseo Neptuno 6 ▪ 963 710 366 ▪ €€

This vast, touristy paella restaurant has been serving up rice dishes for over 120 years and has received a number of famous visitors.

Diners at La Pepica

10 La FABrica
MAP G5 ▪ c/del Cristo del Grao 14 ▪ 960 642 843 ▪ Closed Mon ▪ €

This bar-restaurant is a fun place for tapas with an international twist, plus hearty burgers and platters of local cheeses and charcuterie.

See map on p108

🔟 Beyond the City

The Autonomous Region of Valencia takes in much more than just the city of Valencia itself: the market gardens of La Huerta, the craggy mountains that form the Sierra Calderona, the pretty wetlands in the Parque Natural de la Albufera and wine regions such as Utiel-Requena all lie within an hour's drive of the centre. Other worthwhile sights include Roman castles, monasteries dating back to the 13th-century Christian Reconquest and ceramics towns. Buses run to some of the villages within La Albufera, and trains serve the historic town of Xàtiva. Those

Late-15th-century plate made in Manises

with their own form of transport, though, can see several of the region's sights in an easy day trip, or can stay overnight to make the most of sampling the region's wonderful wines.

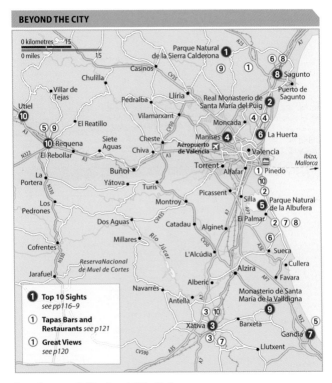

BEYOND THE CITY

Top 10 Sights see pp116–9

Tapas Bars and Restaurants see p121

Great Views see p120

Preceding pages Walking through Xàtiva Castle

1 Parque Natural de la Sierra Calderona

MAP B5 ▪ https://parquesnaturales.gva.es/es/web/pn-serra-calderona

The flat fields north of Valencia gradually give way to the foothills of the Sierra Calderona, which climbs to 907 m (2,975 ft) at its highest point, El Gorgo. The rugged terrain, covered in a cork forest that harbours wild cats and golden eagles, offers a number of good hiking trails within easy reach of the city.

2 Real Monasterio de Santa Maria del Puig

MAP B5 ▪ c/Lo Rat Penat 1A, Puig ▪ 961 470 200 ▪ Tours in English at 10am, 11am, noon, 4pm & 5pm Tue–Sat ▪ Adm ▪ www.monasteriodelpuig.org

The Royal Monastery of Our Lady of El Puig is a powerful symbol of the Reconquest of Valencia. Jaume I believed that his troops had been protected during the Battle of El Puig in 1237 by an image of the Virgin Mary, discovered on this hill (puig in Valencian) a few years before. The king proclaimed the statue patron saint of his new kingdom and ordered a church be built on the spot of his decisive victory. The current Gothic church was constructed on top of this original church in 1300, and an impressive monastery was added in 1588. Guided tours take in the cloisters, the Royal Hall and the church, whose main chapel still contains the statue of the Virgin.

3 Xàtiva

Historic Xàtiva is half an hour by train from the Estación del Nord. Its medieval centre is dotted with Gothic churches, leafy plazas and tempting tapas bars. Visitors should set aside most of their time for the impressive castle overlooking the Old Town, a stronghold used by both the Carthaginians and the Romans (see pp38–9).

4 Manises

MAP B5 ▪ www.manisesturismo.es

Much of the finest tilework seen decorating various buildings around Valencia comes from Manises, a small town by Valencia's airport, where the fine tradition of making metallic-glazed ceramics dates back more than 700 years. Manises tiling is historically blue and white, and there are some superb examples to be seen on the houses along Paseo Guillermo de Osma and on the façade of the town's tourist office.

5 Parque Natural de la Albufera

This fabulous natural park begins not long after you leave the city's southern limits. As well as its vast central lake and ecologically important wetlands, there are beaches, docks lined with wooden boats and several traditional villages in which to tuck into paella from rice grown in the surrounding fields (see pp36–7).

Exploring the wetlands of the Parque Natural de la Albufera by boat

6 La Huerta
MAP B5

The highly fertile fields of La Huerta hold a near-mythical status among Valencianos. Extending immediately north of the city, they have been farmed since Roman times, although it was the Moors who developed the ingenious network of *accequias* (irrigation channels) that funnel water from the Río Turia to feed the crops of potatoes, aubergines, tomatoes, melons and tiger nuts. It is a hypnotic landscape of neat market gardens, olive groves and orchards, dotted with a few grand *alquerías* (farmhouses) and the steep-pitched *barracas* (cabins) that were favoured by workers.

7 Palau Ducal
MAP C6 ■ c/Duc Alfons el Vell 1, Gandia ■ Open 10am–2pm & 4–8pm Mon–Sat, 10am–2pm Sun ■ Adm ■ www.palauducal.com

The deceptively simple exterior of Gandia's Gothic palace belies the extravagance within. Built in the late 13th century, it originally served as the residence of the Royal Dukes of Gandia before being acquired by the Borja (Borgia) family in 1485 – San Francisco de Borja was born here. It later passed into the hands of the Jesuits, its current owners. The halls are the highlights, particularly the tiled Salón de Coronas, with its ornate wooden ceiling, along with the lavish Baroque Galería Dorada and the Neo-Gothic chapel, whose blue vaulted ceiling is covered in gold stars.

8 Castillo de Sagunto
MAP B5 ■ c/Castillo, Sagunto ■ 962 617 267 ■ Open 10am–6pm Tue–Sat (Jun–Sep: to 8pm Sat), 10am–2pm Sun

The ruined castle that wiggles for almost 1 km (0.5 mile) through the foothills of the Sierra Calderona is the most impressive of several Roman remains

A loggia at Castillo de Sagunto

in and around the town of Sagunto. After the Romans left, the castle was used by the Visigoths, Moors and Christians. Remains from the Roman and Muslim periods can best be seen in the Plaza de Armas, home to the Roman forum, and the Plaza de la Conejera, though there is little in the way of information.

9 Monasterio de Santa María de la Valldigna
MAP B6 ■ Plaza de Guillem Agulló, Simat de la Valldigna ■ Opening hours vary, check website ■ https://monestirvalldigna.gva.es

The Monastery of Santa María de la Valldigna was founded by Jaume I in 1298. Its name is said to derive from a conversation the king had with the abbot of Santes Creus: when asked whether the valley was worthy of a monastery, the abbot replied "*Vall digna!*" ("Valley worthy!"). He was right, as the surrounding fertile lands provided the monastery with the economic power to play an active role in Valencian society for almost 600 years – Rodrigo Borgia was abbot here on his way to becoming Pope Alexander VI. The most impressive part of the monastery

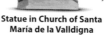

Statue in Church of Santa María de la Valldigna

today is the beautiful Church of Santa Maria de la Valldigna, with six separate chapels, all impressive in their own right, as well as large domes and a wonderfully decorated ceiling.

⑩ Utiel-Requena
MAP A5 ■ DO Utiel-Requena: www.utielrequena.org; Ruta del Vino: www.rutavino.com

Viticulture in Utiel-Requena, which is the largest wine area within the Autonomous Region of Valencia, dates back to the Iberians, 2,500 years ago. The Denominación de Origen takes its name from the neighbouring towns of Utiel and Requena, around 70 km (43 miles) west of Valencia. A network of caves runs beneath both, which were once used to store jars of wine. An organized wine route, the Ruta del Vino, includes several vineyards open for tastings.

THE WINES OF VALENCIA

Valencia is home to three Denominación de Origen wines. In the northwest, DO Utiel-Requena wines are dominated by the native Bobal variety – try Murviedro, in Requena's central square, for a classic example of its earthy, black-fruit flavour. DO Valencia produces dry whites, using Macabeo and Merseguera grapes, and the sweet Moscatel de Valencia. DO Alicante, in the far south, is best known for its Fondillon.

A WINE TOUR OF UTIEL-REQUENA

▶ MORNING

It's recommended visitors hire a designated driver in order to appreciate this tour linking the two towns of the **Utiel-Requena** wine region fully, as it includes stops at a couple of lovely rural wineries. Start on foot in Requena with an introduction to the region's wines at the Museo del Vino in the 15th-century Palace of El Cid (open from 10:30am, closed Mon & Tue; adm €2). Then venture underground to explore the Old Town's Cavas de la Villa – atmospherically lit caverns dug into the limestone during the Moorish era. **Mesón de la Villa** (see p121), one of few lunchtime options in Requena, is very good.

AFTERNOON

After filling up on tapas, set off for Bodegas Chozas Carrascal (https://chozascarrascal.com), a trendy vineyard 18 km (11 miles) northeast of Requena. Guided tours of their stylish modern finca (estate) include a stroll among the vines and tastings of some of their 11 different varieties. Push on towards Utiel, and after 8 km (5 miles) you'll come to Vera de Estenas Bodegas y Viñedos (www.veradeestenas.es), one of the region's most traditional producers. Tours around the vineyards, the family museum (located in a Modernista building dating from 1919) and cellars end with tastings of their highly regarded Bobal wines. Drive on into Utiel for dinner, and finish the day with a glass or two at the bar of time-warped **Café Salón Pérez** (c/Santa María 17).

See map on p116 ←

Great Views

Mirador del Garbí, with great views

Norte. It is located among tiger nut fields, accessed off a cycle lane from the village of Almaràssa.

5 La Fortaleza de Requena
MAP A5 ■ Cuesta del Castillo ■ 962 303 851 ■ Open 10:30am–noon & 7–8pm Tue–Sun ■ Adm

The Torre del Homenaje, Requena castle's 15th-century tower, enjoys the best views in town. Its lower floors are home to a multimedia interpretation centre.

6 Muntanyeta dels Sants
MAP B5

Rising in the middle of the flat Parque Natural de la Albufera, this tree-covered "little mountain" is crowned by a hermitage dedicated to St Abdón and St Senén, traditionally the protectors of crops against hailstorms.

1 Mirador del Garbí
MAP B5

The lookout at this rocky bluff in the eastern ranges of the Parque Natural de la Sierra Calderona offers superb views down over Sagunto and out to the Mediterranean.

2 Mirador del Pujol
MAP B5

Located at the head of the Gola del Pujol, an artificial channel that connects La Albufera lake *(see pp36–7)* to the sea, this mirador (viewpoint) offers uninterrupted views across the water; it is a superb spot at sunset. Boat trips leave from here throughout the day.

3 Torre de Santa Fe
MAP B6

Climb up to the highest point of Xàtiva Castle *(see pp38–9)* for sweeping panoramas across the town's tiled rooftops to the mountains beyond.

4 Alquería de Tomás el d'Aurrèlit
MAP B5

This Andalucian-style farmhouse, owned by the Lladró family, is one of the best-preserved in La Huerta

7 Camino de Cova Negra
MAP B6 ■ www.xativaturismo.com/cova-negra

Neanderthal remains were found in the so-called Black Cave just outside Xàtiva, but it is the walk there, along the Río Albaida and across a rocky ravine, that provides the best views.

8 Plaza de la Ciudadella
MAP B5

From the edge of this square, the largest of seven enclosures in Sagunto's castle, is a great view of the old Roman town below.

9 Mirador de Rebalsadors
MAP B6

This lookout is next to the mountain of the same name, one of the highest peaks in the Sierra Calderona. The scenery is majestic, pine forests flowing all the way down to the sea.

10 La Mallada del Quarter
MAP B5

Occupying the northern end of La Devesa, this *mallada* (dune slack) floods in winter and is a good place to spot some of the park's birds.

Tapas Bars and Restaurants

PRICE CATEGORIES

For a three-course meal for one with half a bottle of wine (or equivalent meal), taxes and extra charges

€ under €35   €€ €35–60   €€€ over €60

1 Llar Roman
MAP B5 ■ c/del Río, Pinedo 258 ■ 963 248 982 ■ €€

Pinedo is just south of Valencia's port, so it is not too far to go to enjoy the fantastic paellas at this esteemed restaurant.

2 Pasqualet
MAP B5 ■ Francisco Monleón 12, El Palmar ■ 961 620 341 ■ Closed D, Mon–Thu ■ €

Located in the centre of El Palmar, this restaurant is a good choice for a paella Valenciana, one with chicken, rabbit and snails.

3 El Túnel
MAP B6 ■ c/Portal Valencia 22, Xàtiva ■ 962 288 237 ■ Closed winter: Mon ■ €

Guests need to knock on the door to enter this tapas bar, which offers unusual plates like lamb filo parcels and mushroom croquettes.

Paella dish at El Sequer de Tonica

4 Barraca Toni Montoliu
MAP B5 ■ Partida de l'Ermita, Meliana ■ 629 689 805 ■ Closed Mon & Tue ■ €€

Toni's farmhouse restaurant offers an insight into La Huerta life. Share a huge paella, then take a horse and carriage ride around the farm.

5 Restaurante Telero
MAP C6 ■ c/San Ponç, Gandia ■ 962 867 318 ■ Closed Sun ■ €€

This charming little restaurant is hidden down a side street in Gandia,

but it's worth seeking out – dishes include *fideuá (see p65)* and Iberian pork with fig sauce.

6 Andana Aljibe
MAP B5 ■ c/de los Dolores 1, Sagunto ■ 667 530 077 ■ Closed Wed ■ €

The best place to eat after visiting Sagunto's castle, this whitewashed restaurant with exposed brickwork is set at the junction of two pretty cobbled streets. It serves great-value three-course menus.

7 Arrocería Maribel
MAP B5 ■ c/Francisco Monleón 5 ■ www.arroceriamaribel.com ■ €€

Diners can choose classic paellas and other rice dishes with chicken, rabbit and lobster or go for more creative fare at this elegant restaurant.

8 El Sequer de Tonica
MAP B5 ■ c/de los Redolins 85, El Palmar ■ 961 620 224 ■ Closed Tue ■ €€

It is hard to go wrong with one of the dozen varieties on offer at this airy restaurant at the end of El Palmar, the historic home of paella.

9 Mesón la Villa
MAP A5 ■ Plaza de Albonoz, Requena ■ 960 302 132 ■ Closed Mon ■ €€

Meat, including *güeña*, a spicy local sausage, dominates the menu at this restaurant on Requena's main square.

10 La Borda de Lola
MAP B6 ■ c/de la Reain 13, Xàtiva ■ 960 707 277 ■ Closed Mon–Thu ■ www.labordadelola.com ■ €€

An interesting menu of creatively prepared dishes makes this one of the best options in Xàtiva.

See map on p116 ←

Streetsmart

Wicker baskets and wooden goods at a shop on Plaza del Mercado

Getting Around

Arriving by Air

Valencia Airport is 8 km (5 miles) west of the city. The Main Terminal (T1 and T2) handles international flights, while domestic flights use the Regional Aviation Terminal. Two metro lines link the airport with the city centre in about 25 minutes: line 3 and line 5. The Metrobus (No 150) departs from outside the T1 Arrivals Hall every half an hour or so. Taxis take at least 20 minutes and cost around €25. There is a tourist information office in the T1 Arrivals Hall.

Direct flights serve Valencia from nine airports in the UK and Ireland, including Gatwick, Heathrow, Manchester, Edinburgh, Belfast and Dublin. There are no direct flights from North America, so US and Canadian visitors could fly to Barcelona, Madrid or Málaga and pick up a domestic flight or a train.

Arriving by Sea

The **Port of Valencia**, 5.5 km (3.5 miles) east of the city centre, operates regular passenger ferry services to and from the Balearic Islands (Ibiza, Menora and Mallorca). Cruise ships dock at nearby Poniente Pier, which is connected to the main port terminal by a free shuttle bus.

Regional and Local Trains

Valencia's main railway terminus is **Joaquín Sorolla Station**, 1 km (0.6 mile) south of the city centre. **Renfe**'s high-speed AVE trains connect Joaquín Sorolla with Madrid, Barcelona, Seville and Córdoba. The station has a tourist information office and is linked to Estación de Norte, on the edge of the Centro Histórico, by a shuttle bus; other parts of the city are accessed by metro lines 1 and 5 from Jesús station, 250 m (820 ft) away.

Local trains (cercanías) to Xàtiva, Gandía and Utiel depart from **Estación del Norte**. Xàtiva metro station (lines 3 and 5) is just outside the railway station's main entrance, and numerous buses run to and from nearby Plaza del Ayuntamiento.

Long-Distance Buses

FlixBus runs services from Paris to Valencia's Estación de Autobuses, just north of the Jardín del Turia, near Turia metro station (line 1). Journey times can be longer than the train but ticket prices are lower if you book ahead.

Driving to Valencia

It takes two days to drive from the UK to Valencia, either via the cross-channel ferry or the Channel Tunnel. The motorway down Spain's Mediterranean coast, the AP-7 (part of the E15), is the fastest way to reach Valencia from France. The N340, once the longest road in Spain, is much slower. The A-3 connects Valencia with Madrid. Always make sure that your car is equipped with two warning triangles and a reflective jacket in case of a roadside emergency.

Public Transport

Sightseeing and getting around Valencia is best done on foot, by bike or by public transport. **EMT Valencia** runs the city's bus system, while **Metrovalencia** runs the metro and tram network. Safety and hygiene measures, timetables, ticket information and transport maps can be obtained online or via the handy EMT app.

Tickets

The Suma 10 ticket, valid for ten journeys on public transport, is the most economical way of getting around and costs from €8. Tickets must be stamped at the beginning of each journey on the metro. Single tickets on buses and the metro cost €1.50. Travel on the metro is free for children under 10.

The **Valencia Tourist Card** offers unlimited journeys on the entire public transport network (including buses) for 24 hours (€15), 48 hours (€20) or 72 hours (€25). The card can be bought at the airport, tourist information offices, Joaquín Sorolla Station or online.

Metro

Metro services operate from 4am to 11:30pm on weekdays and 5am to

12:30am at weekends. The six metro lines and four tram lines are colour-coded, but it is important to know which direction of travel is needed and the name of the end station. The metro system covers four zones, though most visitors are only ever likely to need a ticket for Zone A, except when going to the airport, which is in Zone B.

Buses

The red EMT buses operate within Valencia from 4am to 10:30pm; night buses run from 10:30pm to 2am, and until 3:30am at weekends. Yellow **Fernan** buses serve the suburbs, Manises and the airport. Bus 25 runs from Plaza Puerto de la Mar to Pinedo, and on to El Saler and El Palmar in the Parque Natural de la Albufera.

Taxis

City taxis are white and can be hailed or hired at a taxi rank (a green light indicates that they are free). They can also be booked online, by phone or via an app. Companies include **Tele Taxi Valencia** and **Radio Taxi Valencia**.

Driving in Valencia

Hiring a car in Valencia is unnecessary unless planning a trip to the more remote sights outside the city. There are offices of key car hire companies such as **Auto Europe** and **Enterprise** in the airport and at Joaquín Sorolla Station. Stick to the speed limit: 120 km/h (75 mph) on motorways, 100 km/h (62 mph) on dual carriageways, 90 km/h (56 mph) on single-lane roads and 50 km/h (31 mph) in built-up areas. Try to park in an underground car park; if you park on the road, note that blue markings on the street generally mean you have to buy a ticket from a parking meter. Visitors should be aware that Spain has strict rules on drink-driving.

Cycle Hire

A growing network of cycle lanes connects most of Valencia and extends out into La Huerta and Parque Natural de la Albufera; maps are available from the tourist office. Ciclocalles, streets where bicycles have priority, are also increasing in number. There are numerous bike rental shops, such as **Valencia Bikes**, several of which allow drop-off at a different location. The city has also introduced a bike-sharing system, **Valenbisi**; though aimed at residents it also offers a one-week subscription option for tourists.

Walking

With a compact historic centre and most of its attractions within walking distance from each other, Valencia is a easy city to explore on foot. The huge Jardín del Turia (pp22–3) offers a leafy route right through the city.

DIRECTORY

ARRIVING BY AIR

Valencia Airport
W aena.es

ARRIVING BY SEA

Port of Valencia
W valenciaport.com

REGIONAL AND LOCAL TRAINS

Estación del Norte
c/Xátiva 24
W renfe.com

Joaquín Sorolla Station
c/San Vicente Mártir 171
C 91 232 03 20

Renfe
W renfe.com

LONG-DISTANCE BUSES

FlixBus
W flixbus.es

PUBLIC TRANSPORT

EMT Valencia
W emtvalencia.es

Metrovalencia
W metrovalencia.es

TICKETS

Valencia Tourist Card
W visitvalencia.com

BUSES

Fernan
W fernanbus.es

TAXIS

Radio Taxi Valencia
W radiotaxivalencia.es

Tele Taxi Valencia
W teletaxivalencia.com

DRIVING IN VALENCIA

Auto Europe
W autoeurope.co.uk

Enterprise
W enterprise.co.uk

CYCLE HIRE

Valenbisi
W valenbisi.es

Valencia Bikes
W valenciabikes.com

Practical Information

Passports and Visas

For entry requirements, including visas, consult your nearest Spanish embassy or check the **Exteriores** website. Citizens of the UK, US, Canada, Australia and New Zealand do not need a visa for stays of up to three months but, from 2024, must apply in advance for the European Travel Information and Authorization System (**ETIAS**). Visitors from other countries may also require an ETIAS, so check before travelling. EU nationals do not need a visa or an ETIAS.

Government Advice

Now more than ever, it is important to consult both your and the Spanish government's advice before travelling. The **UK Foreign, Commonwealth & Development Office**, the **US Department of State**, the **Australian Department of Foreign Affairs and Trade** and the Spanish Exteriores website offer the latest information on security, health and local regulations.

Customs Information

For EU citizens, there are no limits on goods that can be taken into or out of Spain, provided they are for personal use. If you are coming from outside the EU, what can be imported depends on whether you are arriving by air and sea or overland; there are no restrictions on exports. You can find information on the laws relating to goods and currency taken in or out of Spain on the **Turespaña** website.

Insurance

We recommend that you take out a comprehensive insurance policy covering theft, loss of belongings, medical care, cancellations and delays, and read the small print carefully. UK citizens are eligible for free emergency medical care in Spain provided they have a valid European Health Insurance Card (EHIC) or UK Global Health Insurance Card (**GHIC**).

Health

Spain has a worldclass healthcare system. Emergency medical care in Spain is free for all UK and EU citizens. If you have an EHIC or GHIC, be sure to present this as soon as possible. You may have to pay after treatment and reclaim the money later.

For visitors coming from outside the UK or EU, payment of medical expenses is the patient's responsibility, so it is important to arrange comprehensive travel insurance before travelling.

For minor ailments, go to a *farmacía* (pharmacy). When closed, they will post a sign giving the location of the nearest pharmacy that will be open. Pharmacies that are open 24 hours include the **Farmacía Plaza España 24h** on Plaza de España. Major hospitals include the **Hospital Universitario y Politécnico de La Fe** and the **Hospital Clínico Universitario**.

For information regarding COVID-19 vaccination requirements, consult government advice.

Smoking, Alcohol and Drugs

Smoking is banned in enclosed public spaces and is a fineable offence, although you can still smoke on the terraces of bars and restaurants.

Spain has a relaxed attitude towards alcohol and it is common to drink on the street outside the bar of purchase.

Recreational drugs are illegal, and possession of even a very small quantity can lead to a hefty fine.

ID

By law you must carry identification with you at all times in Spain. A photocopy of your passport should suffice, but you may be asked to report to a police station with the original document.

Personal Security

Valencia is a generally safe city, but petty crime does take place. Pickpockets work known tourist areas, stations and busy streets. Avoid travelling alone at night on empty streets, particularly in the Barrio del Carmen and El Cabanyal, and leave all valuables in a hotel safe.

The ambulance, police and fire brigade can be called on the Europe-wide **emergency number**. There are also dedicated lines for the **Policía Local** (local police), the **Guardia Civil** (main highways and rural areas) and for **Health Emergencies**.

As a rule, Valencianos are very accepting of all people, regardless of their race, gender or sexuality. Homosexuality was legalized in Spain in 1979 and in 2007 the government recognized same-sex marriage. An array of LGBTQ+ friendly establishments can be found all around the city and the Valencia Gay Pride festival takes place every June.

Travellers with Specific Requirements

Most modern restaurants, hotels, shops, malls and museums are accessible to wheelchair users. Many of the city's older buildings remain inaccessible, so it is always worth calling in advance if you have special requirements. The airport is connected to the city centre by metro lines 3 and 5, both wheelchair accessible. Most city buses have descending ramps and are equipped with technology for the visually impaired. Wheelchair users can also request specially adapted taxis. Metro maps in Braille are available from the Organización Nacional de Ciegos **(ONCE)**.

Valencia also hosts a number of braille reproductions (mini monuments) of places of interest around the city, including La Catedral.

The official tourism website, **Visit Valencia**, features an accessibility guide for those with sensory and accessibility requirements, with lists of accessible hotels and restaurants and detailed information on the city's accessible sights. It also offers audio guides for six routes around the city.

The Confederación Española de Personas con Discapacidad Física y Orgánica **(COCEMFE)** and **Accessible Spain** also provide information and tailored itineraries for those with reduced mobility, sight and hearing.

Time Zone

Spain operates on Central European Time (CET), which is an hour ahead of Greenwich Mean Time (GMT), six hours ahead of US Eastern Standard Time (EST) and nine hours ahead of US Pacific Standard Time (PST). The clock moves forward an hour during daylight savings time, from the last Sunday in March to the last Sunday in November.

DIRECTORY

PASSPORTS AND VISAS

ETIAS
🌐 etiasvisa.com

Exteriores
🌐 exteriores.gob.es

GOVERNMENT ADVICE

Australian Department of Foreign Affairs and Trade
🌐 smartraveller.gov.au

UK Foreign, Commonwealth and Development Office
🌐 gov.uk/foreign-travel-advice

US Department of State
🌐 travel.state.gov

INSURANCE

GHIC
🌐 ghic.org.uk

HEALTH

Farmacía Plaza España 24h
San Vicente Mártir 107, Plaza de España

Hospital Clínico Universitario
Avda de Blasco Ibáñez 17
📞 961 973 500

Hospital Universitario y Politécnico de La Fe
Avda de Fernando Abril Martorell 106
📞 961 244 000

PERSONAL SECURITY

Emergency Number
📞 112

Guardia Civil
📞 062

Health Emergencies
📞 061

Policía Local
📞 092

TRAVELLERS WITH SPECIFIC REQUIREMENTS

Accessible Spain
🌐 accessiblespain travel.com

COCEMFE
🌐 cocemfe.es

ONCE
🌐 once.es

Visit Valencia
🌐 visitvalencia.com/en/Valencia-accesible

Money

The official currency of Spain is the euro (€), which is divided into 100 céntimos.

Cash machines (ATMs) can be found on almost every street corner and are the easiest way to get cash. Spanish banks do not charge a commission for using ATMs, but you will need to check whether your own bank will charge you. Banks tend to offer better exchange and commission rates than bureaux de change.

Spain does not have a big tipping culture, but tipping is appreciated, even rounding up the bill.

Electrical Appliances

Spain uses European plugs with two round pins and the local power supply is 220 volts AC. North American devices will need an adaptor and a voltage converter.

Mobile Phones and Wi-Fi

The country code for Spain is +34. To call abroad from Spain, dial 00, plus the country code, the area code and then the local number.

Most foreign mobile phones will work in Spain, and data roaming can be used on phones from the EU without any additional charges, provided customers do not exceed their monthly allowance. Alternatively, a pay-as-you go local SIM card can be easily acquired.

Free Wi-Fi is readily available in most cafés, hotels and restaurants, and there are dozens of hotspots offering free Wi-Fi that can be accessed across the city.

Postal Services

Post offices are identified by a yellow sign stating **Correos** and are usually open from 9:30am to 8:30pm Monday to Friday and 9:30am to 1pm on Saturday. Suburban and village branches run shorter hours during the week, usually opening 9am to 2pm. Valencia's main post office, a beautiful Neo-Classical building on Plaza del Ayuntamiento (see p51), offers a range of services, including express mail and parcels. Post boxes are painted bright yellow.

Weather

Valencia has a temperate Mediterranean climate, with more than 300 days of sunshine a year. Spring tends to be the best time to visit, when the temperature is comfortable both day and night. Hot summers are freshened by the sea breeze, though the city can get very humid. Autumn can be rainy and winters are mild.

Opening Hours

Shops are usually open from 10am to 2pm and from 5pm to 8pm Monday to Saturday, with many in the city centre also open on Sundays. Larger shops and department stores do not close at lunchtime and are generally open until 9pm. Museums have their own opening hours; many are closed on Mondays. Banks are usually open from 8:30am to 2:30pm Monday to Friday, with a few branches opening on Saturday mornings.

Most banks, stores and businesses close on public holidays: New Year's Day (1 Jan), Epiphany (6 Jan), Feast of San Vicente Mártir (22 Jan), Feast of San José (19 Mar), Good Friday, Easter Monday, Feast of San Vicente Ferrer (5 Apr), Labour Day (1 May), Feast of San Juan (24 Jun), Ascension Day (15 Aug), Day of the Valencian Community (9 Oct), Hispanic Day (12 Oct), All Saints' Day (1 Nov), Constitution Day (6 Dec), Immaculate Conception (8 Dec) and Christmas Day (25 Dec). Some businesses close for the whole of August.

> Situations can change quickly and unexpectedly. Always check before visiting attractions and hospitality venues for up-to-date opening hours and booking requirements.

Visitor Information

The **main tourist office** is well stocked with maps and brochures, provides an accommodation-booking service and sells transport passes, tickets to the main attractions and the discount Valencia Tourist Card (see p124). They can also help with arranging guided tours and bike rental. Other tourist offices are in Joaquín Sorolla Station; on Calle Paz; at Playa de las Arenas; in the port's Passenger Cruise Terminal building; and at the airport.

Free publications can be downloaded from the official tourism website, **Visit Valencia**, including a selection of maps, guides and themed itineraries.

The hop-on, hop-off **Valencia Bus Turístic** operates two routes: Historical Valencia and Maritime Valencia. The tourist office organizes walking and cycling tours around La Huerta and to La Albufera. Valencia Bikes (see p127) runs tours around the Jardín del Turia (see p22–3).

Local Customs

Corridas (bullfights) are held in Valencia. Supporters argue that the bulls are bred for the industry and would be killed as calves were it not for bullfighting, while animal rights organizations frequently hold protests throughout Spain. If you do attend a corrida, bear in mind that it's better to see a big name matador because they are more likely to make a quick kill.

Spain retains a strong Catholic identity: when visiting religious buildings ensure that you are dressed modestly. Most churches and cathedrals will not permit visitors during Sunday Mass.

Responsible Tourism

Named European Green Capital for 2024, Valencia is passionate about sustainable urban development and tourism. The city is also committed to becoming a climate-neutral and smart city by 2030. There are simple ways visitors can help towards these goals: reduce emissions by cycling or walking around the city; embrace locally and sustainably sourced cuisine; and use reusable water bottles and bags when out and about.

Languages

The two official languages are Valencian (related to Catalan) and Spanish (Castilian). While the city council is increasingly promoting Valencian, both languages are used throughout the city – most streets are signposted with their Valencian and Spanish names, and road signs are always bilingual. Some attractions, hotels, restaurants and tapas bars will use the Spanish forms of their address, while others will use the Valencian; confusingly, a few will vary between the two. While some people may prefer to speak Valencian, everyone also speaks Spanish. English is not widely spoken except in hotels and some restaurants. For consistency and clarity, we have used Castilian Spanish throughout this guide with very few exceptions for sights that are only ever officially referred to locally in Valencian.

Taxes and Refunds

IVA in mainland Spain is normally 21 per cent, but with lower rates for certain goods and services. Under certain conditions, non-EU citizens can claim a rebate of these taxes. Present a form and your various receipts to a customs officer at your point of departure.

Accommodation

Accommodation in Spain falls into the following categories: hotels, including paradors, rated between one and five stars; hostals, which are simple guesthouses (not to be confused with youth hostels); youth hostels, generally with dorms; B&Bs; apartments; and student residences, which offer cheap summer stays.

The tourist office provides a database of accommodation. Hotels can be booked through the tourism website or via an online booking portal, such as **Booking.com** and **Hotels.com**, or directly with the hotel.

Book your accommodation well in advance if you plan to visit in the peak season (July and August). Most hotels quote their prices without including tax (IVA), which is 10 per cent in Valencia.

DIRECTORY

POSTAL SERVICES

Correos
w correos.es

VISITOR INFORMATION

Main Tourist Office
Plaza del Ayuntamiento

Valencia Bus Turístic
w valenciabusturistic.com

Visit Valencia
w visitvalencia.com

ACCOMMODATION

Booking.com
w booking.com

Hotels.com
w hotels.com

Places to Stay

PRICE CATEGORIES
For a standard double room per night (with breakfast if included), taxes and extra charges.

€ under €125   €€ €125–250   €€€ over €250

Historic Hotels

Petit Palace Plaza de la Reina

MAP M3 ▪ Carrer de L'Abadia de Sant Martí 3 ▪ www.petitpalace.com ▪ €€

The Valencia branch of this Spanish hotel chain is a small 1930s palace near the city's busy central square. Fresh, bright rooms sleep up to five people (a triple and a bunk bed). They offer a free breakfast if you book via the website.

Hospes Palau de la Mar

MAP P4 ▪ Avda Navarro Reverter 14 ▪ www.hospes.com ▪ €€€

This 19th-century palace in upmarket L'Eixample has spacious rooms done up in minimalist style, either fronting a flower-filled garden or the Jardín del Turia. The swanky on-site Bodyna spa is one of the best in the city.

Hotel Caro

MAP M2 ▪ c/del Almirante 14 ▪ www.carohotel.com ▪ €€€

Superbly located in the heart of the Centro Histórico, just steps from the cathedral, this stylish hotel occupies the former palace of the Marqués de Caro. The rooms, some of which feature sections of the old city walls, have been given a modern makeover.

The Westin Valencia

MAP E4 ▪ Amadeo de Saboya 16 ▪ www.marriott.com ▪ €€€

On the edge of the Jardín del Turia, this grand hotel in a Modernista building boasts spacious Art Deco rooms, three restaurants (two with terraces), a cocktail bar and an excellent spa. Shelter from the bustle of the city in its tranquil garden.

Boutique Hotels

Hotel One Shot Mercat 09

MAP L3 ▪ c/Músico Peydró 9 ▪ www.hoteloneshotmercat09.com ▪ €€

The designers have had fun with this hotel near the Mercado Central, filling the lobby and restaurant with avant-garde art installations. The rooms mix modern and classic styles, with illuminated ceilings that look like frescoes alongside exposed brickwork and wrought-iron balconies.

Marques House

MAP M3 ▪ c/Abadia de Sant Martí 10 ▪ www.marqueshouse.com ▪ €€€

This whitewashed hotel has modern elegant rooms. It's worth paying a bit more for the pared-back superior rooms, which have sitting areas and balconies overlooking the cobbled streets. The city's signature cocktail, Agua de Valencia, is said to have been invented in the hotel's bar.

SH Hotel Boutique Inglés Valencia

MAP M3 ▪ c/del Marqués de Dos Aguas ▪ www.inglesboutique.com ▪ €€

The light, sunny rooms at this hotel are set off a striking atrium whose walls are covered in architectural sketches. Upgrading to a renovated superior room gives guests special views of the Museo Nacional de Cerámica's incredible Baroque façade, which also wows diners eating on the restaurant terrace.

Vincci Lys

MAP M4 ▪ c/Martínez Cubells 5 ▪ www.vinccilys.com ▪ €€€

This chic hotel with very elegant rooms is set on a quite side street in the southern Centro Histórico; it is a short walk from the Plaza del Ayuntamiento and conveniently located for the metro and the main train station.

Vincci Mercat

MAP L3 ▪ c/de la Linterna 31 ▪ www.vinccimercat.com ▪ €€€

Located in the Centro Histórico near the Mercado Central, this smart, concept hotel has 68 modern double rooms, tastefully decorated in muted earthy browns and whites. Some rooms have adjoining doors, and extra beds are available. The rooftop plunge-pool is an unusual bonus for such a convenient location.

Design Hotels

MD Design Hotel
MAP M2 ■ c/Boix 3
■ www.hotelesmd.com
■ €
Located in the Centro
Histórico district of La
Seu, this is an urban
design hotel in the
minimal, beechwood
Scandinavian sense of
the word. There are good
views of the Jardín del
Turia from the terrace.

Hotel Dimar
MAP P5 ■ Gran Via del
Marqués del Túria 80
■ www.hotel-dimar.com
■ €€
Graphics and prints of
Valencia's iconic sights
add interest to the modern
rooms of this boutique
hotel in well-heeled
L'Eixample. It is in the
Canovas area, so there
are plenty of fashionable
restaurants and shops in
the surrounding streets.

Alternative Hotels

Casual Valencia Vintage
MAP L4 ■ Plaza del
Ayuntamiento ■ www.
casualhoteles.com ■ €
This novel establishment
is one of five differently
themed Casual hotels in
the city. Retro decor is
the order of the day here,
ranging from old maps
and Vespas to Audrey
Hepburn and Star Wars.

Malcolm & Barret
MAP E6 ■ Avda Ausiàs
March 59 ■ www.hotel
malcomandbarret.com
■ €€
Located in the outlying
district of Quatre Carreres,
this hotel offers good-
value rooms for those
who don't mind being

further from the sights.
A day's bike hire is
included in the rates.

Hotel NH Collection Valencia Colón
MAP M4 ■ c/Colón 32
■ www.nh-collection.com
■ €€€
The eye-catching interior
of this 19th-century building, the work of Spanish
designer Lorenzo Castillo,
includes a black-and-
white sci-fi lobby and
India-inspired rooms. It
is close to the restaurants
in the Mercado de Colón.

Hotels by the Beach

Hotel Balandret
MAP H5 ■ Paseo Neptuno
22 ■ www.balandret.com
■ €€
Enjoying a super setting
on Playa de las Arenas's
beachfront promenade,
this elegant hotel has very
good-value rooms and
unique public spaces, full
of ceramic-tile murals
and wall art made from
botijos (clay water jars).

Neptuno
MAP H5 ■ Paseo Neptuno
2 ■ www.hotelneptuno
valencia.com ■ €€
Right behind Playa de
las Arenas and next to
the marina, this convivial
hotel is a great place to
enjoy the Mediterranean
lifestyle. Rooms have
splashes of marine
colours while public
areas have interesting
works of art.

Hotel Las Arenas Balneario Resort
MAP H4 ■ Eugenia Viñes
22–24 ■ www.hotel
valencialasarenas.com
■ €€€
This large, seafront hotel
began life as a spa in

1898. Decadent pampering
sessions are still a big
draw, as is its location,
directly overlooking Playa
de las Arenas. The paella
restaurants of Paseo de
Neptúno are close by.

Apartments

Barracart
MAP G4 ■ c/de la Barraca
79 ■ www.barracart.com
■ €
In a converted building in
the thick of the old fishing
quarter of El Cabanyal,
these seven apartments
make a lovely retreat from
the streets. They are all
light, whitewashed and
with plenty of exposed
brick. The superior apartments, with balconies, are
great; the duplex ones,
which sleep up to four
people and have their own
terraces, are even better.

Soho Valencia
MAP L6 ■ Gran Via de les
Germanies 32 ■ www.
sohovalencia.com ■ €
A range of smart but
sparse apartments in a
grand-looking building in
the heart of trendy Ruzafa
district, often referred to
as the Valencian Soho.

La Casa del Puerto
MAP G5 ■ Carrer del Pare
Lluís Navarro 3 ■ www.
apartamentoslamas
bonita.es ■ €€
Four very cool apartments
overlook an internal
courtyard at this complex
in El Cabanyal, close to
the beach and with a
tram stop just outside
for easy access to the
Centro Histórico. Run
by the same people
behind La Màs Bonita
Patacona café *(see p112)*,
they have an effortlessly
sylish look and feel.

General Index

Acknowledgments

This edition updated by

Contributor Mary-Ann Gallagher

Senior Editors Dipika Dasgupta, Alison McGill

Senior Art Editor Vinita Venugopal

Project Editors Anuroop Sanwalia, Lucy Sara-Kelly

Art Editor Bandana Paul

Assistant Editor Ilina Choudhary

Picture Research Administrator Vagisha Pushp

Picture Research Manager Taiyaba Khatoon

Publishing Assistant Simona Velikova

Jacket Designer Jordan Lambley

Senior Cartographer Mohammad Hassan

Cartography Manager Suresh Kumar

Senior DTP Designer Tanveer Zaidi

DTP Designer Rohit Rojal

Senior Production Editor Jason Little

Senior Production Controller Samantha Cross

Managing Editors Shikha Kulkarni, Beverly Smart, Hollie Teague

Managing Art Editor Sarah Snelling

Senior Managing Art Editor Priyanka Thakur

Art Director Maxine Pedliham

Publishing Director Georgina Dee

DK would like to thank the following for their contribution to the previous editions: Hilary Bird, Keith Drew, Debra Wolter

The publisher would like to thank the following for their kind permission to reproduce their photographs:

Key: a-above; b-below/bottom; c-centre; f-far; l-left; r-right; t-top

123RF.com: Olena Kachmar 81b.

Alamy Stock Photo: AA World Travel Library 38cl; Action Plus Sports Images 54cl; age fotostock 72crb, / Gonzalo Azumendi 11crb, 26bl, 52tl, 66b, 110bl, 117b, / Historical Views 116tl, / Nacho Moro 37cr, / Pietro Scozzari 98tl; Jerónimo Alba 39tl; Art Collection 4 11tl, 33bl; Gonzalo Azumendi 10crb, 61b, 63bl, 72tl, 91cr, 104t, 109br; Suzy Bennett 18clb; Bruce yuanyue Bi 48bc, 94cla; Philip Bird 16bl; Michael Brooks 20cl; Joaquin Corbalan pastor 69cl; Cavan Images / Aurora Photos / Katja Heinemann 29tl; Ian Dagnall 103br; Oscar Dominguez 70br; Josie Elias 68br; 118bc; Ana Escobar 60c; Robert Evans 96tl; Peter van Evert 10cr, 17bl, 44tc; Faraway Photos 6cla, 10cla, 12–13c, 50clb, 61tl, 89cl; Foto Espana 86cla; Kevin Foy 34br; 51tr; Eddie Gerald 35crb; Vlad Ghiea 11cr; Hemis.fr / Gardel Bertrand 28tl, / Giuglio Gil 84tl, / Hughes Hervé 22clb; Heritage Image Partnership Ltd / Index / Pere Rotger 49tr; Peter Horree 4clb; IanDagnall Computing 33cra; imageBROKER 39cr, / Barbara Boensch 88b, 105cl, 114–15, / Karl F. Schofmann 49cl, 79cl, 106tl, / Marco Simoni ß4cl; Jon Bower- art and museums 27crb; Eddie Linssen 4cla, 10bl; Stefano Politi Markovina 18–19c, 26–7c, 51b, 62tl, 87tr, 112tl; Patti McConville 59br; Juan Carlos Munoz 36–7c, 104bl; Jesús Nadal 54br; Peter Noyce ESP 4cr, 26crb; Cum Okolo 7cra, 37tl, 47tr, 55tl, 71clb, 99br, 106br; Mehul Patel 12bl, 15cr; Miguel A. Muñoz Pellicer 14bl; Phil Crean A 100cl; The Picture Art Collection 30cr; PvE 30bc, 31tr, 32tr; Simon Reddy 64cb; Eduardo Ripoll 34cla, 70tl; Robertharding / Neil Farrin 44b; Travelstock44.de / Juergen Held 19tl, 63cr; Lucas Vallecillos 3tl, 3tr, 4t, 4b, 7br, 46t, 48t, 74–5, 110–11tc, 113crb, 122–3; Jan Wlodarczyk 24–5; World History Archive 42cr, 42bl, 43tl; Zoonar / Marco Bonacini 10clb.

Almalibre Açaí Bar: 84cb.

AWL Images: Cahir Davitt 38–9b; Giuglio Gil 67cr; Stefano Politi Markovina 21tl, 46br; Ken Scicluna 2tr, 40–41.

Bombas Gens Centre d'Art: 58tl.

Café ArtySana: 67tl.

Catedral de Valencia: 15tl, 17tr.

Colla Monlleo: 90ca.

Depositphotos Inc: Elephotos 11bl.

Dreamstime.com: Anasife 73tr; Leonid Andronov 29b; Efesan 65tr; Elenaphotos 109t; Giuseppemasci 14–15c; Rostislav Glinsky 23cr; Lunamarina 92–3; Madrugadaverde 52b; Meinzahn 21br; Juan Moyano 13tl, 69tr; Pabkov 20crb; Radub85 71tr, 77tl; Salvacubells 120tl; Stockcreations 121c.

Getty Images: AWL Images / Mark Sykes 28cr; Corbis Historical / Photo Josse / Leemage 30clb; Europa Press News 101crb; Josep Iglesias - fotografia 118–19tc; Lonely Planet Images 108tl, / Krzysztof Dydynski 64tl, 76cla, / Greg Elms 102tl; Moment / Domingo Leiva 96–7b,/ Image by Sherry Galey 19br, / MAIKA 777 56–7; Stringer / Jose Jordan 43br;Quality Sport Images 55br.

Getty Images / iStock: aluxum 53tl; chrisdorney 45tl; fotoVoyager 47cl; Jorgefontestad 35tl, 37b; Sergdid 2tl, 8–9; Siempreverde22 22bc; Sloot 78t, 95cr; to_csa 68t.

IVAM Institut Valencià d'Art Modern: 13cr.

La Postalera: 82clb.

Mercado de Tapineria: 80tl.

Nozomi Sushi Bar: 65cl.

Radio City: 83cr.

Robert Harding Picture Library: Hugh Rooney 11cb.

Shutterstock: Alexey Fedorenko 1; Riccardo Cirillo 22-23c; trabantos 20bl, 77br.

Tavella Restaurant: 107cr.

Trinquet de Pelayo: 58b.

Ubik Cafe: 4crb.

Cover
Front and Spine: **Shutterstock.com:** Alexey Fedorenko
Back: **Alamy Stock Photo:** Ian Dagnall cla, Giuseppe Masci tr; **iStockphoto.com:** aluxum crb; Lucas Vallecillos tl; **Shutterstock.com:** Alexey Fedorenko b

Pull Out Map Cover
Shutterstock.com: Alexey Fedorenko

All other images are: © Dorling Kindersley. For further information see www.dkimages.com.

First edition 2020

Published in Great Britain
by Dorling Kindersley Limited
DK, One Embassy Gardens, 8 Viaduct Gardens, London SW11 7BW, UK

The authorised representative in the EEA is Dorling Kindersley Verlag GmbH. Arnulfstr. 124, 80636 Munich, Germany

Published in the United States by
DK Publishing, 1745 Broadway, 20th Floor, New York, NY 10019, USA

A CIP catalogue record for this book is available from the British Library.

A catalogue record for this book is available from the Library of Congress.

ISSN 1479-344X

ISBN 978 0 2416 6368 4

Printed and bound in Malaysia

www.dk.com

As a guide to abbreviations in visitor information blocks: **Adm** *= admission charge;* **D** *= dinner.*

MIX
Paper | Supporting responsible forestry
FSC™ C018179

This book was made with Forest Stewardship Council™ certified paper – one small step in DK's commitment to a sustainable future.
For more information go to www.dk.com/our-green-pledge

Phrase Book: Castilian

In an Emergency

Help!	¡Socorro!	soh-koh-roh
Stop!	¡Pare!	pah-reh
Call a doctor.	¡Llame a un médico!	yah-meh ah oon meh-de-koh
Call an ambulance.	¡Llame a una ambulancia!	yah-meh ah ahm-boo-lahn-thee-ah
Call the police	¡Llame a la policía!	yah-meh ah lah poh-lee-three-ah
Call the fire brigade.	¡Llame a los bomberos!	yah-meh ah lohs bohm-beh-rohs

Communication Essentials

Yes/No	Sí/No	see/noh
Please	Por favor	pohr fah-vorh
Thank you	Gracias	grah-thee-ahs
Excuse me	Perdone	pehr-doh-neh
Hello	Hola	oh-lah
Goodbye	Adiós	ah-dee-ohs
Good night	Buenas noches	bweh-nahs noh-chehs
What?	¿Qué?	keh?
When?	¿Cuándo?	kwan-doh?
Why?	¿Por qué?	pohr-keh?
Where?	¿Dónde?	dohn-deh?

Useful Phrases

How are you?	Cómo está usted?	koh-moh ehs-tah oos-tehd
Very well, thank you.	Muy bien, gracias.	mwee bee-ehn grah-thee-ahs
Pleased to meet you.	Encantado/a de conocerle.	ehn-kahn-tah-doh deh koh-noh-thehr-leh
That's fine.	Está bien.	ehs-tah bee-ehn
Where is/are …?	¿Dónde está/están?	dohn-deh ehs-tah/ehs-tahn
Which way to …?	¿Por dónde se va a …?	pohr dohn-deh seh bah ah
Do you speak English?	¿Habla inglés?	ah-blah een-glehs
I don't understand.	No comprendo.	noh kom-prehn-doh
I'm sorry.	Lo siento.	loh see-ehn-toh

Shopping

How much does this cost?	¿Cuánto cuesta esto?	kwahn-toh kwehs-tah ehs-toh
I would like …	Me gustaría …	meh goos-ta-ree-ah
Do you have …?	¿Tienen …?	tee-yeh-nehn
Do you take credit cards?	¿Aceptan tarjetas de crédito?	ah-thehp-than tahr-heh-tas-deh kreh-deee-toh
What time do you open/close?	A qué hora abren/cierran?	ah keh oh-rah ah-brehn/thee-ehr-rahn
this one/that one	éste/ése	ehs-teh/eh-seh
expensive	caro	kahr-oh
cheap	barato	bah-rah-toh
size (clothes)	talla	tah-yah
size (shoes)	número	noo-mehr-oh
white	blanco	blahn-koh
black	negro	neh-groh
red	rojo	roh-hoh
yellow	amarillo	ah-mah-ree-yoh
green	verde	behr-deh
blue	azul	ah-thool

bakery	la panadería	lah pah-nah-deh-ree-ah
bank	el banco	ehl bahn-koh
bookshop	la librería	lah lee-breh-ree-ah
cake shop	la pastelería	lah pahs-teh-leh-ree-ah
chemist	la farmacia	lah fahr-mah-thee-ah
grocer's	la tienda de comestibles	lah tee-yehn-dah deh koh-mehs-tee-blehs
hairdresser	la peluquería	lah peh-loo-keh-ree-ah
market	el mercado	ehl mehr-kah-doh
newsagent	el kiosko de prensa	ehn kee-ohs-koh deh prehn-sah
supermarket	el super-mercado	ehl soo-pehr-mehr-kah-doh
travel agency	la agencia de viajes	lah ah-hehn-thee-ah deh bee-ah-hehs

Sightseeing

art gallery	la galería de arte	lah gah-leh-ree-ah deh ahr-teh
bus station	la estación de autobuses	lah ehs-tah-ee-ohn deh owtoh-boo-sehs
cathedral	la catedral	lah kah-teh-drahl
church	la iglesia/la basílica	lah ee-gleh-see-ah/lah-bah-seel-i-kah
closed for holidays	cerrado por vacaciones	thehr-rah-doh porhr bah-kah-cee-oh-nehs
garden	el jardín	ehl hahr-deen
museum	el museo	ehl moo-seh-oh
railway station	la estación de trenes	lah ehs-tah-thee-ohn deh treh-nehs
tourist information	la oficina de turismo	lah oh-fee-thee-nah deh too-rees-moh

Staying in a Hotel

Do you have any vacant rooms?	¿Tienen una habitación libre?	tee-eh-nehn oo-nah ah-bee-tah thee-ohn lee-breh
double room	Habitación doble	ah-bee-tah-thee-ohn dob-bleh
with double bed	con cama de matrimonio	kohn kah-mah deh mah-tree-moh-nee-oh
twin room	Habitación con dos camas	ah-bee-tah-thee-ohn kohn dohs kah-mahs
single room	Habitación individual	ah-bee-tah-thee-ohn een-dee-vee-doo-ahl
room with a bath/shower	Habitación con baño/ducha	ah-bee-tah-thee-ohn kohn bah-nyoh/doo-chah
I have a reservation.	Tengo una habitación reservada.	tehn-goh oo-na ah-bee-tah-thee-ohn reh-sehr-bah-dah

Eating Out

Have you got a table for …?	¿Tienen mesa para … ?	Tee-eh-nehn meh-sah pah-rah

I'd like to reserve a table.	**Quiero reservar una mesa.**	kee-eh-roh reh-sehr-bahr oo-nah meh-sah
breakfast	**el desayuno**	ehl deh-sah-yoo-noh
lunch	**la comida/ el almuerzo**	lah koh-mee-dah/ehl ahl-mwehr-thoh
dinner	**la cena**	lah theh-nah
The bill, please.	**La cuenta, por favor.**	lah kwehn-tah pohr fah-vohr
waiter/waitress	**camarero/ camarera**	kah-mah-reh-roh/ kah-mah-reh-rah
fixed-price menu	**menú del día**	meh-noo dehl dee-ah
dish of the day	**el plato del día**	ehl plah-toh dehl dee-ah
starters	**los entremeses**	lohs ehn-treh-meh-sehs
main course	**el primer plato**	ehl pree-mehr plah-toh
wine list	**la carta de vinos**	lah kahr-tah deh bee-nohs
glass	**un vaso**	oon bah-soh
bottle	**una botella**	oon-nah boh-teh-yah
knife	**un cuchillo**	oon koo-chee-yoh
fork	**un tenedor**	oon the-neh-dohr
spoon	**una cuchara**	oon-ah koo-chah-rah
coffee	**el café**	ehl kah-feh
rare	**poco hecho**	poh-koh eh-choh
medium	**medio hecho**	meh-dee-oh eh-choh
well done	**muy hecho**	mwee eh-choh

Menu Decoder

al horno	**ahl ohr-noh**	baked
asado	**ah-sah-do**	roast
el aceite	**ah-thee-eh-teh**	oil
aceitunas	**ah-theh-toon-ahs**	olives
el agua mineral	**ah-gwa mee-neh-rahl**	mineral water
sin gas/con gas	**seen gas/ kohn gas**	still/sparkling
el ajo	**ah-hoh**	garlic
el arroz	**ahr-rohth**	rice
el azúcar	**ah-thoo-kahr**	sugar
la carne	**kahr-ne**	meat
la cebolla	**theh-boh-yah**	onion
la cerveza	**thehr-beh-thah**	beer
el cerdo	**thehr-doh**	pork
el chocolate	**choh-koh-lah-the**	chocolate
el chorizo	**choh-ree-thoh**	red sausage
el cordero	**kohr-deh-roh**	lamb
el fiambre	**fee-ahm-breh**	cold meat
frito	**free-toh**	fried
la fruta	**froo-tah**	fruit
los frutos secos	**frooh-tohs seh-kohs**	nuts
las gambas	**gahm-bas**	prawns
el helado	**eh-lah-doh**	ice cream
el huevo	**oo-eh-voh**	egg
el jamón serrano	**hah-mohn sehr-rah-noh**	cured ham
el jerez	**heh-reh**	sherry
la langosta	**lahn-gohs-tah**	lobster
la leche	**leh-cheh**	milk
el limón	**lee-mohn**	lemon

la limonada	**lee-moh-nah-dah**	lemonade
la mantequilla	**mahn-teh-kee-yah**	butter
la manzana	**mahn-thah-nah**	apple
los mariscos	**mah-rees-kohs**	shellfish
la menestra	**meh-nehs-trah**	vegetable stew
la naranja	**nah-rahn-hah**	orange
el pan	**pahn**	bread
el pastel	**pahs-tehl**	cake
las patatas	**pah-tah-thas**	potatoes
el pescado	**pehs-kah-doh**	fish
la pimienta	**pee-mee-yehn-tah**	pepper
el plátano	**plah-tah-noh**	banana
el pollo	**poh-yoh**	chicken
el postre	**pohs-treh**	dessert
el queso	**keh-soh**	cheese
la sal	**sahl**	salt
las salchichas	**sahl-chee-chahs**	sausages
la salsa	**sahl-sa**	sauce
seco	**seh-koh**	dry
el solomillo	**soh-loh-mee-yoh**	sirloin
la sopa	**soh-pah**	soup
la tarta	**tahr-ta**	tart
el té	**teh**	tea
la ternera	**tehr-neh-rah**	beef
las tostadas	**tohs-tah-dahs**	toast
el vinagre	**bee-nah-gre**	vinegar
el vino blanco	**bee-noh blahn-koh**	white wine
el vino rosado	**bee-noh roh-sah-doh**	rosé wine
el vino tinto	**bee-noh teen-toh**	red wine

Numbers

0	**cero**	theh-roh
1	**un/una**	oon-noh/oon-uh
2	**dos**	dohs
3	**tres**	trehs
4	**cuatro**	kwa-troh
5	**cinco**	theen-koh
6	**seis**	says
7	**siete**	see-eh-teh
8	**ocho**	oh-choh
9	**nueve**	nweh-veh
10	**diez**	dee-ehth
11	**once**	ohn-theh
12	**doce**	doh-theh
13	**trece**	treh-theh
14	**catorce**	kah-tohr-theh
15	**quince**	keen-theh
16	**dieciseis**	dee-eh-thee-seh-ess
17	**diecisiete**	dee-eh-thee-see-eh-teh
18	**dieciocho**	dee-eh-thee-oh-choh
19	**diecinueve**	dee-eh-thee-newh-veh
20	**veinte**	beh-een-teh
30	**treinta**	treh-een-tah
40	**cuarenta**	kwah-rehn-tah
50	**cincuenta**	theen-kwehn-tah
60	**sesenta**	seh-sehn-tah
70	**setenta**	seh-tehn-tah
80	**ochenta**	oh-chehn-tah
90	**noventa**	noh-vehn-tah
100	**cien**	theh-ehn
1000	**mil**	meel
1001	**mil uno**	meel oo-noh

Phrase Book: Valencian

In an Emergency

Help!	Auxili!	ow-gzee-lee
Stop!	Pareu!	pah-reh-oo
Call a doctor!	Telefoneu un metge!	teh-leh-fon-eh-oo oom meh-djuh
Call an ambulance.	Telefoneu una ambulància!	teh-leh-fon-eh-oo oo-nah ahm-boo-lahn-see-ah
Call the police.	Telefoneu la policia!	teh-leh-fon-eh-oo lah poh-lee-see-ah
Call the fire brigade.	Telefoneu los bombers!	teh-leh-fon-eh-oo lohs bohm-behrs

Communication Essentials

Yes/No	Sí/No	see/noh
Please	Si us plau	si us plau
Thank you	Gràcies	grah-see-uhs
Excuse me	Perdoni	puhr-thoh-nee
Hello	Hola	oh-lah
Goodbye	Adéu	ah-they-oo
Good night	Bona nit	bo-nah neet
Yesterday	ahir	ah-ee
Today	avui	un-voo-ee
Tomorrow	demà	duh-mah
What?	Què?	keh?
When?	Quan?	kwahn
Why?	Per què?	puhr keh
Where?	On?	ohn

Useful Phrases

How are you?	Com està?	kom uhs-tah
Very well, thank you.	Molt bé, gràcies.	mol beh grah-see-uhs
Pleased to meet you.	Molt de gust.	mod duh goost
That's fine.	Està bé.	uhs-tah beh
Where is/are …?	On és/són …?	ohn ehs/sohn
Which way to …?	Per on es …?	puhr on uhs
Do you speak English?	Parla anglès?	par-luh an-glehs
I don't understand	No l'entenc.	noh luhn-teng
I'm sorry.	Ho sento.	oo sehn-too

Shopping

How much does this cost?	Quant costa això?	kwahn kost ehs-shoh
I would like …	M'agradaria …	muh-grah-thuh-ree-ah
Do you have …?	Tenen …?	tehn-un
Do you take credit cards?	Accepten targetes de crèdit?	Ak-sehp-tuhn tahr-guh-tuhs duh kreh-deet
What time do you open/close?	A quina hora obren/tanquen?	Ah keen-uh oh-bruhn/tan-kuhn
this one/that one	aquest/aquell	Ah-ket/Ah-kehl
expensive	car	kahr
cheap	bé de preu/barat	be thuh preh-oo/bah-rat
size (clothes)	talla/mida	tah-lyah/mee-thuh
size (shoes)	número	noo-mehr-oo
white	blanc	blang
black	negre	neh-gruh
red	vermell	vuhr-mel
yellow	groc	grok
green	verd	behrt
blue	blau	blah-oo
bakery	el forn	uhl forn
bank	el banc	uhl bang

bookshop	la llibreria	lah lyee-burh-ree-ah
cake shop	la patisseria	lah pahs-tee-suh-ree-uh
chemist	la farmàcia	lah fuhr-mah-see-ah
grocer's	la botiga de queviures	lah boo-tee-guh duh kee-vee-oo-ruhs
hairdresser's	la perruqueria	lah peh-roo-kuh-ree-uh
market	el mercat	uhl muhr-kat
newsagent	el quiosc de premsa	uhl kee-ohsk duh prem-suh
supermarket	el supermercat	uhl soo-puhr-muhr-kat
travel agency	l'agència de viatges	la-jen-see-uh duh vee-ad-juhs

Sightseeing

art gallery	la galeria d'art	lah gahl-uh-ree-yah dart
bus station	l'estació d'autobusos	luhs-tah-see-oh dow-toh-boo-zoos
cathedral	la catedral	lah kuh-tuh-thrahl
church	l'església/la basílica	luhz-gleh-zee-uh/lah buh-zee-lee-kuh
closed for holidays	tancat per vacances	tan-kat puhr bah-kan-suhs
garden	el jardí	uhl zhahr-dee
museum	el museu	uhl moo-seh-oo
railway station	l'estació de tren	luhs-tah-see-oh thuh tren
tourist information	l'oficina de turisme	loo-fee-see-nuh thuh too-reez-muh

Staying in a Hotel

Do you have any vacant rooms?	Tenen una habitació lliure?	teh-nuhn oo-nuh ah-bee-tuh-see oh lyuh-ruh
double room	habitació doble	ah-bee-tuh-see-oh dohbluh
with double bed	amb llit de matrimoni	am lyeet duh mah-tree moh-nee
twin room	habitació amb dos llits/amb llits individuals	ah-bee-tuh-see-oh am dohs lyeets/am lyeets in-thee-vee-thoo-ahls
single room	habitació individual	ah-bee-tuh-see-oh in-thee-vee-thoo-ahl
room with a bath/shower	habitació amb bany/dutxa	ah-bee-tuh-see-see-oh am bahnyou/doo-chuh
I have a reservation.	Tinc una habitació reservada.	Ting oo-nuh ah-bee-tuh-see-oh reh-sehr-vah-thah

Eating Out

Have you got a table for …?	Tenen taula per … ?	teh-nuhn tow-luh puhr
I'd like to reserve a table.	Voldria reservar una taula.	Vool-dree-uh reh-sehr-vahr oo-nuh tow-luh
breakfast	l'esmorzar	les-moor-sah
lunch	el dinar	uhl dee-nah
dinner	el sopar	uhl soo-pah

The bill, please.	el compte, si us plau.	uhl kohm-tuh sees plah-oo
waiter/waitress	cambrer/ cambrera	kam-breh/kam-breh-ruh
fixed-price menu	menú del dia	muh-noo duhl dee-uh
dish of the day	el plat del dia	uhl plat duhl dee-uh
starters	els entrants	uhlz ehn-tranz
main course	el primer plat	uhl pree-meh plat
wine list	la carta de vins	lah kahr-tuh thuh veens
glass	un got	oon got
bottle	una ampolla	oo-nuh am-pol-yuh
knife	un ganivet	oon gun-ee-veht
fork	una forquilla	oo-nuh foor-keel-yuh
spoon	una cullera	oo-nuh kool-yeh-ruh
coffee	el café	ehl kah-feh
rare	poc fet	pok fet
medium	al punt	ahl poon
well done	molt fet	mol fet

Menu Decoder

l'aigua mineral	lah-ee-gwuhl mee-nuh-rah-rah	mineral water
sense gas/ amb gas	sen-zuh gas/ am gas	still/ sparkling
l'all	lahlyuh	garlic
al forn	ahl forn	roasted
l'arròs	lahr-roz	rice
les botifarres	lahs boo-tee-fah-rahs	cured meats
la carn	lah karn	meat
la ceba	lah seh-buh	onion
la cervesa	lah-sehr-ve-seh	beer
el filet	uhl fee-let	sirloin
el formatge	uhl for-mah-djuh	cheese
l'embotit	lum-boo-teet	cold meat
fregit	freh-zeet	fried
la fruita	lah froo-ee-tah	fruit
els fruits secs	uhlz froo-eets seks	nuts
les gambes	lahs gam-bus	prawns
el gelat	uhl djuh-lat	ice cream
la llagosta	lah lyah-gos-tah	lobster
la llet	lah lyet	milk
la llimona	lah lyee-moh-nah	lemon
la llimonada	lah lyee-moh-nah-thuh	lemonade
la mantega	lah mahn-teh-gah	butter
el marisc	ulh mur-reesk	seafood
la menestra	lah muh-nehs-truh	vegetable stew
el pa	uhl pah	bread
el pastís	uhl pahs-tees	pie/cake
les patates	lahs pah-tah-tuhs	potatoes
el peix	pehs-kah-doh	fish
el pebre	pee-mee-yehn-tah	pepper
el pernil	uhl puhr-neel	cured ham
el plàtan	uhl plah-tun	banana
el pollastre	uhl puu-lyah-struh	chicken
la poma	lah poh-mah	apple
el porc	uhl pohr	pork
les postres	lahs pohs-truhs	desserts
rostit	rohs-teet	roast
la sal	lah sahl	salt
les salsitxes	lahs sahl-see-chuhs	sausages
la salsa	lah sahl-suh	sauce

sec	sehk	dry
el sucre	uhl soo-kruh	sugar
la taronja	lah tuh-rohn-djuh	orange
el te	uhl teh	tea
les torrades	lahs too-rah-thuhs	toast
la vedella	lah veh-theh-lyuh	beef
el vi blanc	uhl bee blang	white wine
el vi negre	uhl bee neh-greh	red wine
el vi rosat	uhl bee roo-zaht	rosé wine
el xai/el be	uhl shahee/ uhl beh	lamb
la xocolata	lah shoo-koo-lah-tuh	chocolate

Numbers

0	zero	zeh-roh
1	un/una	oon/oon-uh
2	dos/dues	dohs/doo-uhs
3	tres	trehs
4	quatre	kwa-truh
5	cinc	seeng
6	sis	sees
7	set	set
8	vuit	voo-eet
9	nou	noh-oo
10	deu	deh-oo
11	onze	on-zuh
12	dotze	doh-dzuh
13	tretze	treh-dzuh
14	catorze	kah-tohr-dzuh
15	quinze	keen-zuh
16	setze	set-zuh
17	disset	dee-set
18	divuit	dee-voo-eet
19	dinou	dee-noh-oo
20	vint	been
21	vint-i-un	been-tee-oon
30	trenta	tren-tah
40	quarenta	kwuh-ran-tuh
50	cinquanta	seen-kwahn-tah
60	seixanta	seh-ee-shan-tah
70	setanta	seh-tan-tah
80	viutanta	voo-ee-tan-tah
90	noranta	noh-ran-tah
100	cent	sen
101	cent un	sen oon
1000	mil	meel
1001	mil un	meel oo-noh

The following words crop up frequently in maps and on street signs. You may encounter them in their Castilian or Valencian forms, depending on which part of Valenica and its environs you are visiting.

English	Castilian	Valencian
Avenue	Avenida	Avinguda
Beach	Playa	Platja
Cape	Cabo	Cap
Castle	Castillo	Castell
Market	Mercado	Mercat
Museum	Museo	Museu
Square	Plaza	Plaça
Street	Calle	Carrer
Town Hall	Ayuntamiento	Ajuntament